the PAPER BRIDE

Esther K. Smith

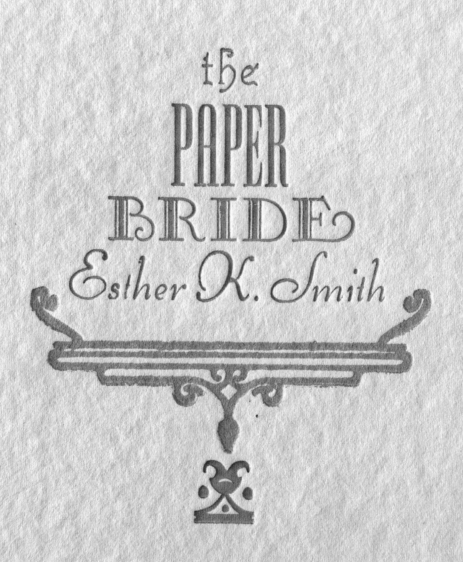

THE PAPER

POTTER
CRAFT

NEW YORK

Wedding D·I·Y from Pop-the-Question to Tie-the-Knot and Happily Ever After

BRIDE

by Esther K. Smith

illustrations: **Liz Zanis**

photography: **Amy Kalyn Sims**

type-o-graphic illos: **Dikko Faust**

You Rang?

FOR THE GROOM'S EYES ONLY

Save the Date!

THE PLEASURE OF YOUR COMPANY

Boys Allowed!

TIE THE KNOT

EAT, DRINK & BE MARRIED

HAPPILY EVER AFTER

Introduction
Weddings in Purgatory

"*A ll brides go insane,*" *I said.*

The *New York Times* reporter's ears pricked up.

"*——in a positive way.*"

The reporter wrote the story, just a few short paragraphs with pictures of a few of our wedding invitations, and we were in high gear (as high as you can get when you hand-set metal and wood type for every letter of every word).

A bride and groom found us from there. They were getting married in Grand Central Station (which we learned to call Terminal). We got together and brainstormed—decided to design their invitations based on an old subway token, had paper handmade with a watermark based on our design. (I began to want to clone certain couples who were so much fun to work with.) We made coasters for them, large die-cut vintage subway tokens. The MTA gift-shop manager visited. She loved them. And a few years later, I saw they had done their own version of the idea—but not letterpress on absorbent coaster board, some plastic version.

A woman called from *Manhattan User's Guide:* "I hear you make the way coolest wedding invitations in New York City." (Way coolest??—it brought me back to playground, fourth grade.) But of course—we did.

How had all this happened?

{ **Purgatory Pie Press coasters and our invitation with my crazy handmade envelope.**

Dikko had gone to grad school at the University of Wisconsin-Madison to study with Walter Hamady and learn typography and letterpress printing. He wanted to make a book with his friend Tim's poems. That was his third book. In the meantime, he had become the letterpress printer at New York City's Center for Book Arts. And when friends got married, he would make their invitations—as well as business cards and gallery announcements for people who happened to walk in.

I was living in Chicago then, designing for theater, and getting cold—really, really cold. My raincoat froze in my closet and started peeling like a sunburn. Dikko called me.

"OK," he said.

"What?"

"Let's get married."

"Let me check something. I'll call you back."

I called our friend Mikey and asked if he would brew homemade ginger beer with champagne yeast for the wedding. He said yes.

So I called Dikko back and said,

"OK."

Miss Manners says you need to have a certain number of fights before a wedding. Dikko and I had different friends in college—so naturally our first fight about the guest list started right away. The only thing we agreed on was that we'd have a RED wedding (to both our mothers' dismay).

Our invitation was our first letterpress collaboration. I've been designing wedding invitations and the things that accompany them ever since.

⌐ **Purgatory Pie Press invitation, die-cut and hand-set metal type.**
Purgatory Pie Press coaster, hand-set metal type. }

$\mathcal{M}$y dad was an organist when I was very little. I have hazy memories of lovely, lacy brides. (And also a lady named Violet who wore a mink stole with a head that bit its tail.) When I was bigger we would go to see plays at a place called Allenberry, where they served sticky pecan buns in their dinner breadbaskets. People had weddings there and the veiled white brides and their pale pastel-frocked attendants were the fairy princesses among the hummingbirds and sweet-smelling hollyhocks in their old-fashioned gardens. I knew I would have my wedding there.

Things changed. A 1968 *Romeo & Juliet* movie inspired Wanamaker's department store to show a wedding party in gorgeous brown and bronze silks. I gasped when I saw it with my aunt. She said if I graduated from college before getting married she would buy me a wedding dress.

But we had a very different wedding. My father had died. My aunt didn't remember (always get those promises in writing!). I couldn't imagine having my mother pay for a wedding. And, as young artists, Dikko and I couldn't afford it. But there was so much we could do ourselves. I was a costume designer. We found Dikko a bowler hat and tails in vintage shops. I did wear a dress from my aunt, one she had given me for dress-ups when I was little, a bias-cut silk velvet gown from the 1920s. I'd kept it up with safety pins, so had to mend a hole in the bodice.

Whether you are having an elaborate formal wedding or the simplest small ceremony, you can make it your own. You can do these projects on a clean kitchen table with a pair of sharp scissors and a few simple tools. You can work with fancy expensive handmade paper or go green and recycle bridal magazines. You can make some things in minutes—if you are more ambitious, others could take weeks. And you might take comfort in the stress release of folding papers and lining envelopes and addressing your envelopes in your own beautiful handwriting. (See handwriting guide, page 132.)

After the intensity of a wedding, marriage is a breeze. We've celebrated our silver anniversary! (Time flies when you're having fun!)

Here's to doing it yourself
& Happily Ever After.

— Esther

Eat Drink November 6 *Bert & Betty* 1954 and Be Married

Prologue
Proposal

FOR THE GROOM'S EYES ONLY

The phone rang.

"Hello, would you be able to letterpress one copy of a book of poems?"

"Printing a single copy of a book letterpress is possible, but it's very expensive—all the hand typesetting and press setups for one copy."

"My girlfriend and I live in different cities, so I have been reading her poems on the phone. I want to make those into a book to give her when I ask her to marry me with an heirloom diamond ring (on the full moon, in the Rockies)—"

"If she says yes, you must come to us for your invitations—"

We did NOT print that book letterpress. Our intern set the type on a computer and laser-printed it on all rag business paper. Then we had our bookbinder add pages, carve a hole, and insert a ring box.

He gave her the book. She was thrilled. The ring caught the light of the full moon. And she did say yes, and we made them beautiful invitations and coasters with nine different poems.

{ Georgia Luna collaged this book (opposite and page 13).

Secret Hidden Ring Box Book

In the 1960s English artist Tom Phillips went looking for a cheap used book with good paper and a strong binding. He found a Victorian novel: *A Human Document*. He painted and collaged the pages and unwrote it, removing words, and parts of words, reducing it into his own text. He called it *A Humument*. It became his life's work—I saw an exhibit of new pages from it a few years ago—and last I checked, it was in its fourth revised edition.

What book would you like to sacrifice for this ring box? It's your choice. A classic? Something in print? Or browse through a used bookstore for a book that catches your eye.

At the Center for Book Arts in New York City, there was an old French book about the size of a pocket paperback that hides a pack of playing cards, which were illegal when the book was made.

For your Secret Hidden Ring Box Book, follow Tom Phillips's example and choose a nice strong binding, and paper that isn't yellowed or brittle. But whether it's her favorite Jane Austin or a romance novel or something you've never seen before, be sure that it is thick enough to hold the ring box. See if you can find a book that comes with a nice slipcase . . .

Materials

HARDBACK BOOK *that is bigger than the ring box*

PENCIL

UTILITY KNIFE

METAL STRAIGHTEDGE OR TRIANGLE

GLUE AND/OR DOUBLE-STICK TAPE

PHOTOS, COLLAGE MATERIALS *(optional)*

BONE FOLDER

RING BOX + ENGAGEMENT RING!

1 Open your book so that the height of the back half is a little taller than your ring box.

2 With your straightedge, lightly trace the outline of ring box on the top page of the back half of the book, in the center of the page.

3 With your knife, use the outline to cut a channel through to the back of the book. The channel should be deep enough to hold your box. You may have to cut in several sections or even just a few pages at a time. This part takes time and patience.

4 Glue the box to the back cover of the book.

5 If you'd like, à la Phillips, embellish the book with collage or even add poems and photos that have significance.

If you add anything, you need to remove some thickness, so the book will close square. It would seem to make sense to just tear out entire pages, but that would affect the whole binding. You need to cut or tear out the pages close to the spine, but leave a little margin, a finger's width or so—use a straightedge and knife and protect the sheets underneath with a piece of cardboard or a cutting mat. Or tear, if you like that look—but leave a bit of the page close to the spine so the stitching is left intact.

Once you have removed some of the thickness, you can collage onto the remaining sheets or even turn them into a photo album. If you use wet glue or media (like watercolor), make sure that you dry the book under weight with clean waste sheets. (Waste sheets can be any one-sided pieces of printing paper from your recycle pile.) As these sheets become damp, you exchange them for dry ones—when the damp ones dry you can put them back in to absorb more.

NOTE: *This technique of interleaving waste sheets and changing them is also a way to rescue books that you've dropped in the tub (or left out in the rain) . . .*

To avoid the waste-sheets technique, use double-stick tape (you can get sheets of it) or a nonwrinkling glue stick. Choose photo-safe adhesives so your book will last for years without yellowing.

Burnish your additions well with a bone folder, protecting their surface with a clean waste sheet— bone folders leave a shine on paper if you use them directly—though silicone "bone" folders don't—but the silicone ones cost more—about five times as much— so I haven't invested in one.

Another groom came to us after he'd secretly followed his beloved to Paris when she went there for a business trip, carrying a ring engraved with "Paris Toujours." Illustrator Jane Sanders made an illustration of that ring. We printed it in different sizes on the save-the-dates, invitations, even coasters. It became their brand. He even had us print it on some handmade paper that he retrieved a year later for a first anniversary gift.

Instead of an engagement ring, consider engagement bling. Ryan Murphy designed and had this one made for his bride-to-be (with a solid-gold safety-pin closure!). Anchors became a motif after they found one on their first road trip together.

5.5

Cinco-de-Mayo

NICOLE
&
NOAH

will be wed in a
simple Buddhist
ceremony

Wat Fai Hin
Chiang Mai
Thailand

In Thai: 55=haha

Save the Date!

Chapter 1
Engagement

A re you a June bride?
Or do you love autumn leaves more than pink roses?

October was always my favorite month, so I knew I wanted to have our wedding then. Though my mother-in-law offered to organize a June wedding in her garden. As you choose your date, you have a few things to consider. Does it make sense to do it when school's out, so that teachers and students and people with kids can travel? Maybe there is a holiday like Halloween or Valentine's Day that you'd like to always celebrate as your anniversary. And where do you want to have your wedding? If it's in June, you will need to reserve far in advance. An Irish bride told me that only one hotel in her town was considered proper for weddings, so they would have to reserve four years in advance. Hopefully you have more flexibility!

You have so many decisions to make—how large will your wedding be? Dinner? Dancing? What's your budget? What are your families' traditions? Are you paying for things yourself or are your parents or families paying all or part? In Chinese weddings the groom's family pays—in American weddings the bride's family pays—if a Chinese woman marries an American man—well, you need to work out these details. (This was the case with some friends of ours—they paid for their own wedding.) How about attendants? What colors will they wear? And flowers, the caterer—all those business cards!

{ **Purgatory Pie Press, hand-set wood and metal type on hand-made paper. Nicole Gilbo took the photo of Chiang Mai.**

one story has haunted the hearts of its readers. It is "Green Mansions," the story of Rima, the girl of strange beauty and Abel, the adventurer...who met and loved in a jungle Eden where menace lurked amid the orchids.

Determined to turn the W. H. Hudson story into visual and musical sorcery,

M-G-M trekked a troupe 25,000 miles to pierce the luxuriant jungles of Venezuela. They enlisted the musical genius of Brazilian composer Villa-Lobos and the ritual choreography of Katherine Dunham. No wonder the screen sends out a kaleidoscope of magnificent sights, mystery and mood.

Audrey Hepburn, as if born for the role of Rima, captures all the fragile loveliness of the exquisite, untouched girl of the forest. And Anthony Perkins is equally right as the adventurous and romantic Abel who finds his life's most amazing experience in the jungle.

With him, you go into a virginal jungle paradise. You share his excitement as he discovers Rima, a stranger to civilization. And in this dreamlike Eden he pursues her, tasting sweet, wild, tumultuous love. But evil lurking in every Eden, here takes the shape of superstition and threatens the young lovers with hate and violence.

Characterizations you'll remember are Lee J. Cobb as the sinister Nufflo, Sessue Hayakawa as the native chief and Henry Silva as the vengeful warrior.

For this entertainment wrought in dazzling Metrocolor and CinemaScope, credit

Paper Pocket Planner

Now you are engaged. There is so much to do. Where do you start? You need an organizational system. Make yourself a wedding planner!

Brides bring me swatches as they figure out their color schemes and begin to think about flowers and attendants' dresses. It's nice to have something to store them in. This book is based on a narrow accordion, or "concertina," spine. It has pockets for brochures, receipts, fabric swatches, menus, and magazine clippings, or anything that inspires you visually. Make it big enough to hold your wedding invitation, but small enough to throw in your bag.

As you choose envelopes, papers, cloth, and buttons, let your personal taste work for you. Are you attracted to white and silver or creams and subtle neutrals?

Do you prefer olive green and celadon? Pastels or dark colors? Or do you like an interesting contrast, like sky blue and brown or pink and gray? Do you love ribbons and lace, silks and satins? Or are soft cottons or crisp linens appealing to you? Relax—enjoy this process. You will begin feeling your way into the mood of your whole wedding.

NOTE: *I'm specifying standard, letter-size business paper because it's so easy to find—but it's your choice. You can make this whatever size works best for you.*

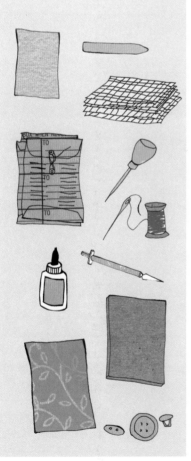

Materials

STRONG, FOLDABLE COVER-WEIGHT PAPER *(could be Tyvek) to make the concertina spine—about the same height that you choose for your interior pages—it could be a little smaller or larger*

BONE FOLDER

LETTER-SIZE GRAPH PAPER *for interior pages (assorted graphs can make an interesting look, depending on your taste)—another type of letter-size lightweight paper would also work*

9" X 12" (23 X 30.5 CM) ENVELOPES—*could be glassine or interoffice—or something else that you think looks good*

AWL

NEEDLE AND LINEN THREAD

SCISSORS OR X-ACTO KNIFE

WHITE GLUE AND BRUSH OR DOUBLE-SIDED TAPE

BOARD FOR COVERS—*mat board or museum boards or bookbinding board—approximately 6" x 9" (15 x 23 cm)—you should wait until you make the inside of the book before you cut it, to be sure the cover is big enough*

SANDPAPER *to smooth rough edges of board, if necessary*

BOOK CLOTH *or strong opaque paper (optional—if you'd like to cover your boards—directions follow)*

BUTTONS, ELASTIC *(optional)*

WASTE SHEETS

COVER-WEIGHT END-SHEET PAPER—*plain or patterned (optional)*

{ Lissi Erwin made her wedding planner (opposite and pages 20 and 21).

1. Take your piece of cover-weight paper and fold it in half horizontally, burnishing (as always) with your bone folder. Fold each half in half, and fold each of those sections in half. Then reverse folds as necessary to make a narrow concertina (a smaller accordion!). This will form the spine of your organizer book.

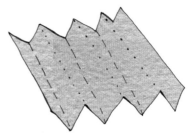

2. Look at your folds. Some go up—alternate folds go down. In origami terms, the ones that go up are "mountains" and the opposite folds are "valleys." You will sew your folded sections into the valleys.

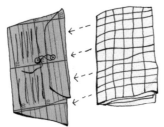

3. For each section, or "signature" in bookbinding lingo, lightly fold the envelope in half horizontally, so that it measures approximately 6" x 9" (15 x 23 cm). Take four to eight sheets of graph paper, either the same pattern or assorted, and lightly fold them horizontally, place the folded paper inside the fold of the envelope, and burnish with your bone folder.

4. Line up the signatures in the valleys of your concertina spine. Remember that your covers will attach to the outer pieces of the concertina. Punch sewing holes with your awl. Pierce through the fold of your signatures into the spine fold. Make three holes, one near the top, one near the bottom, and one in the middle.

5. Sew the signature with envelope to the spine with what's called a pamphlet stitch (see page 111). Stitch in a B shape—out through the middle, leaving a long tail, in through the top or bottom, skip the middle, out through the top or bottom, back in the middle. Adjust the tension—pulling with care so your thread doesn't rip through your paper. Tie a square knot, left over right, right over left AROUND the long stitch, and it won't be able to pull through.

6. One side of your envelope will be closed. Slit the top of this side so that you can tuck things—receipts, swatches, menus—inside.

You can glue additional, smaller envelopes to the mountains if you like.

7 Cut your covers 6" x 9" (15 x 23 cm), or a bit larger, from the mat board or museum board. A framer may be happy to sell you insides of mats cheap (or even give them to you). You can smooth the edges with sandpaper if necessary. If you like, cover these boards with book cloth or paper (instructions below). Glue the front and back cover to the outer pieces of your accordion spine. You can line your cover with a decorative endpaper—cut it a bit smaller than the cover, if you want to hide the hinge.

8 For a closure, you can punch holes with an awl and attach a button or two to the front cover—and attach a long thread to the button to tie around the book and wrap around the button.

OR make an elastic loop big enough to go around the whole front cover. Punch two holes in the back cover and thread elastic big enough to go around the book. Tie the elastic with a square knot—you can leave this exposed on the inside or hide with a smaller piece of decorative card stock or an end sheet—a piece of contrasting or decorative paper used to hide the "works" in most bookbinding (see what we used to line the cover here)!

To Cover Boards

You can cover your boards with book cloth or paper—you will be able to use this technique with other projects.

1 Cut your book cloth larger than the covers on all sides. It's easy to cut with scissors or an X-Acto knife.

2 Center the board on the cloth and glue down.

3 Fold the cloth over the board on all sides and burnish to crease.

4 Trim the corners, leaving enough cloth to cover the board thickness.

5 Glue the top and bottom.

6 Glue the sides.

7 Work corners with your bone folder to be sure your boards are covered and to flatten the cloth at the corners.

8 Adhere the boards to your accordion and then line the insides with end sheets made from cover-weight paper.

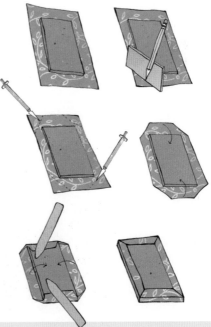

NOTE: You can even pad your cover with felt or quilt stuffing—pull your fabric around on all sides and adhere it to the back (a bit like upholstering a chair seat).

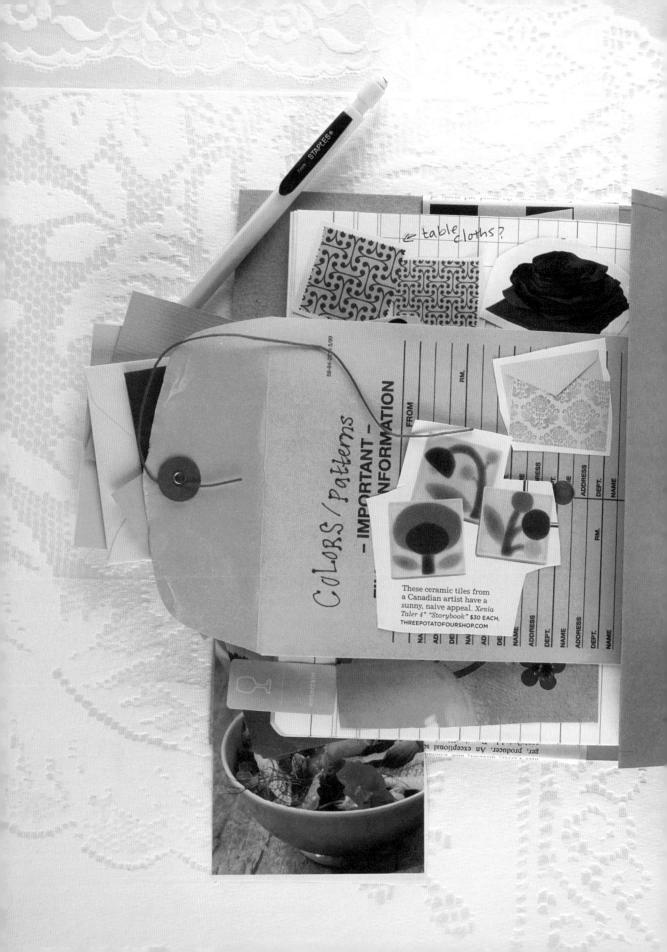

Savannah ~ River

Locations

Use Until All Spaces Are Filled

Gilbert's favorite location to set up camp is the Kenya-Tanzania border near Lake Natron (pictured), where she met her fiancé.

ONDENCE

beautiful
TO AQUAMARINE
BLUE

vintage wall phone
Landlines are falling out of fashion, but this would add such a cool old-school touch to the kitchen. Western Electric #2554 $70 OLDPHONES.COM

Pool at Vogue in the 1960s.

The Lake, Prospect Park, Brooklyn, N.Y.

POST CARD

THIS SPACE FOR ADDRESS ONLY

PLACE
ONE CENT
STAMP
HERE

SAVE THAT DATE!

FELICITY ERWIN
&
RYAN MURPHY

OCTOBER II, 2009

The Grand
PROSPECT PARK BOATHOUSE
BROOKLYN, NEW YORK

C. W. HUGHES & CO., INC., MECHANICVILLE, N.

"CORTONE" REG. U.S. PAT. OFF. MADE ONLY BY CURT TEICH & CO., INC., CHICAGO

Gerald + Sarah Murphy
6949 Nichols Lane
Cincinnati, OH 45202

Save-the-Date Postcard

How much time do you have before your wedding? How far will people need to travel to attend? Do you want to send something before your invitation? You may need a save-the-date. (Or you could just use it to announce your engagement.)

Choose a style. Do you want a postcard with a picture or just words? This first communication can let people know how formal your wedding will be. It also shows people your taste and sense of style— the first impression of the couple you will be. Your save-the-date can be as simple as a postcard. If you keep the information cryptic, you don't need to worry about privacy. You could find "Wish You Were Here" location postcards of, say, the Prospect Park Boathouse in Brooklyn— and write: "Felicity Erwin & Ryan Murphy October 11, 2009—Save the Date!"

You could combine it with a holiday card. In January it could be New Year's; a little later, a Chinese New Year's card or a valentine. I saw a sign in a Silcilian pastry shop for Sfingi. It was a gigantic cream puff filled with ricotta, a fat slice of candied orange, plus grated dark chocolate—for St. Joseph's Day, a break from Lent, close to St. Patrick's Day—and Purim. There is always some holiday to celebrate.

Use a baby picture or combine several photos in a montage. Add word balloons with your info. If your info is on the front, use the backs for the addresses. If the front is a picture, put your info text on the left and address the postcards on the right.

You could take a photo of yourselves holding a sign with the date. Set it up like American Gothic—that famous Grant Wood painting of the deadpan man and woman—he's holding a pitchfork. Or look for vintage postcards. One bride found some postcards she liked and realized they had been published by a local pharmacy. It turned out they had plenty left in storage, so she bought a few hundred to use in her invitations.

If you can only find a few vintage cards, you could scan and print or color-photocopy them onto card stock. Check its size and alter it if you need to via computer or by enlarging or shrinking it on a photocopier. I recommend using off-white paper so that the back isn't too bright and jarring. Then, depending on quantity, print or hand-write your info on the back.

At Purgatory Pie Press, Dikko and I worked with a bride who collected postcards and chose a different one for each person she invited—we printed the same info on the backs of all the postcards.

Or try an all-typographic approach. Since Dikko hand-sets real vintage wood and metal type, we often find that is image enough. Your date—like 5/5 or 9/10/11—or your initials, D&E—or FE&RM—can be your central image. This design could be the first piece in a series—so that all your future pieces have a similar look.

greetings from sam and rob

greetings from sam and rob

greetings from sam and rob

greetings from sam and rob

{ Lissi Erwin (opposite) and Liz Zanis (right) made these postcards with computer and laser printer. }

Save-the-Date Postcard

Materials

CARD STOCK

SCRAP PAPER

PRINTER OR PHOTOCOPY MACHINE—*black-and-white or color*

X-ACTO KNIFE OR STRAIGHTEDGE

1 Choose your picture. Write your words.

2 Test your printer—how do you need to feed the paper (or will it print on both sides)? How do different cover-weight papers go through the printer?

3 Fold a piece of standard business paper in quarters. Plan to have two fronts and two backs on each side. Indicate where those will be (you can scribble a simple mock-up front and back on the different quarters) and print a two-sided test on your printer to see how it works.

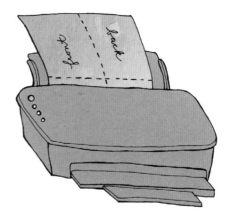

4 Set up both sides based on what you learned from your printer test—then test your real paper to see how it prints. I made a group book project via photocopier with a class. It worked on the standard paper. But the "good" paper didn't print as well. So check all this before you go into production. It can seem slow and frustrating, but it's what the pros do. (I can't begin to tell you how many different proofs the book you are reading went through!) Think of this as a warm-up for your invitation if you end up printing that yourself—your learning curve!

5 Send yourself one to see how it goes through the mail.

6 When you are happy with all your tests—PRINT. Then carefully trim your postcards. Some copy shops have areas where you can use their equipment to cut things down. There are photo trimmers available very cheaply—I got one for 99¢. Or use an X-Acto knife and straightedge. Cut away from yourself! And stock some fingertip Band-Aids just in case.

And stamps!!! You can order stamps with your own picture for a surcharge—only the typography on those usually annoys me—and they have that pesky barcode.

I find stamps that I like at the post office. Michael Bartalos, an artist we collaborated with, has done several postage stamps. They are beautiful and don't cost extra. Postcards postage is less than regular letters, but there are size restrictions which could change when postage goes up. Check the post office website. (Where you can also mail-order interesting stamps that might be hard to find at a post office.)

If your post office has a philatelic window, go there. Friends of ours recommended a post office near Grand Central Station with a clerk who loved helping people with their weddings. He suggested using a variety of old stamps to add up to the right postage.

One of our brides found a vintage stamp dealer who sold her the denominations she needed in stamps that went with her theme (which was New York City sights). They charged extra—but it was worth it. Even if your stamps cost double, it will be a drop in the ocean of the price of your whole wedding—so get what you love.

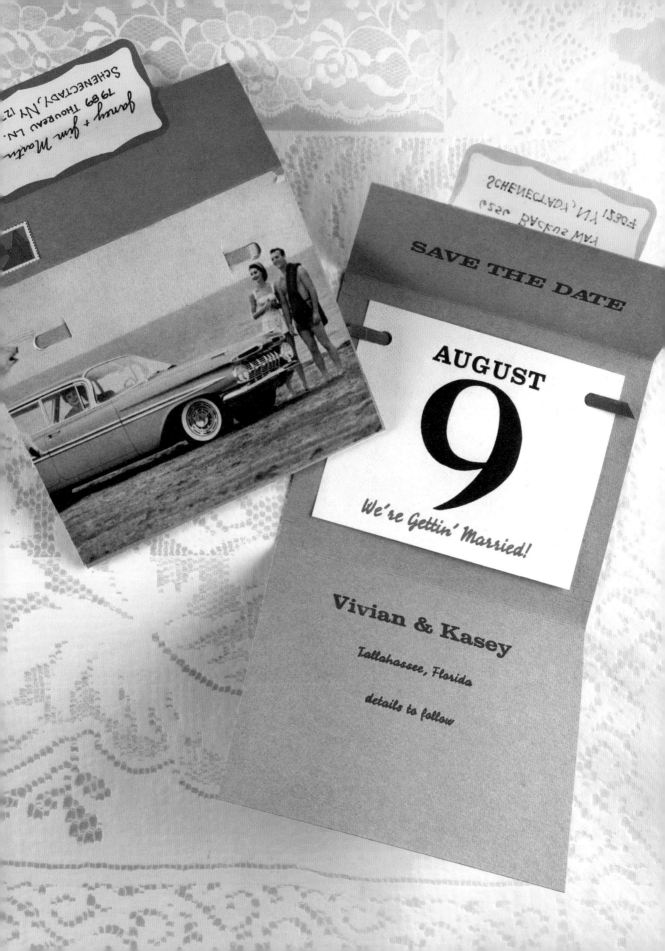

SAVE THE DATE

AUGUST
9

We're Gettin' Married!

Vivian & Kasey

Tallahassee, Florida

details to follow

Self-Mailer

If you would like more privacy than a postcard, but don't want to get involved with envelopes, consider a self-mailer. This could be as simple as a business-size paper flyer folded in thirds and stuck shut with a sticker or piece of tape, stamped and addressed on the outside.

But there are some nicer variations.

Materials

FOLDABLE, HEAVY-WEIGHT PAPER—*big enough to fold into thirds to make into its own envelope—even letter-size paper can work for this*

SCISSORS

TAPE, GLUE, OR STICKER FOR CLOSURE

PRINTER OR PHOTOCOPY MACHINE

BONE FOLDER

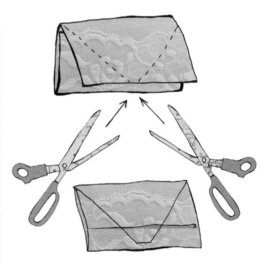

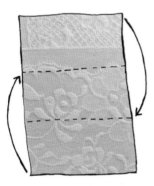

1 Start with the paper—it does need to fold, so check the paper to see that it folds across the horizontal without resistance. To test this, you need to test the paper grain. Bounce the paper in both directions—fold the paper the way it wants to fold—take the path of least resistance—and that's the mystery of figuring out the paper grain!

2 To design, fold your paper so that the top and bottom overlap. Then think about how you'd like to shape the paper. You can cut the corners off the top to make an envelope-style flap. If you make the flap sharp enough, you may want to cut a slip in the bottom flap so that the top flap fits in—but unless you shape the flap to lock into a slit, you'll need to stick it shut with tape, glue, or a sticker.

{ Lissi Erwin designed these; Dikko Faust hand set the metal type.

3 You can print your information on the inside, or add a photo or a card for your text—"float" it on a piece of double-stick tape—or cut slits for the corners to fit.

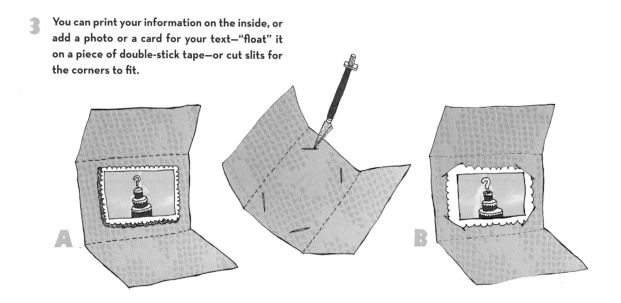

A   B

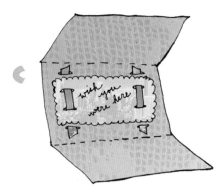

C

If you are printing the inside, you need to use paper that will work with your printer or photocopier—a standard size and texture. If you are inserting a piece that has all the info on it, instead of printing on the mailer, your mailer can be a nonstandard size or of a less even texture. You can cut slots in both the mailer and the piece to be added, and thread them together with a strip of paper "ribbon"—cut its corners at an angle for easier threading—this paper strip could be in a third contrasting color as a nice design element.

4 Seal the top and bottom flaps with a glue stick (burnish well with your bone folder!) or double-stick tape or close with a sticker. You can print or photocopy your return address on the sticker or directly onto the mailer, or put it on with a rubber stamp. And for the mailing addresses—you may want to make a simple computer database and print that out; alternatively, you can type or handwrite onto labels that you will photocopy for various mailings relating to your wedding. We handwrote a mailing list on some interesting labels that we pasted up on a business-size piece of paper. Whenever we needed the addresses, we photocopied the list onto pressure-sensitive sticky-back paper, cut the addresses up, and used them. It has a much more personal look than typical printer labels—and it's only a little more work. Your own handwriting (if it's legible) can be a nice touch because people will recognize it and have an immediate warm response to its familiarity.

Refrigerator Magnet

A refrigerator magnet is a great save-the-date. There are many options for magnets—you can buy pressure-sensitive sticky-back magnets that are easy to cut and can be stuck to anything. There is also magnetic paper now that you can run through a computer printer. You can do a photocopy transfer onto mat board and stick a magnet to the back. Or use balsa wood (though this is the Paper Bride, not the Balsa Wood Bride!). You can even collage or hand-color these.

Photo-transfers reverse your picture—words show up in a mirror image (though you could send your magnet with a pocket mirror. . .). So flip your picture before you print out. A good copy shop can do this for you—or do it on a computer. Photocopies and laser printouts transfer best when they are hot off the press—the fresher the better.

Liz Zanis printed the top and middle on magnetic computer paper. Lissi Erwin laser-print transferred her design on the D+E.

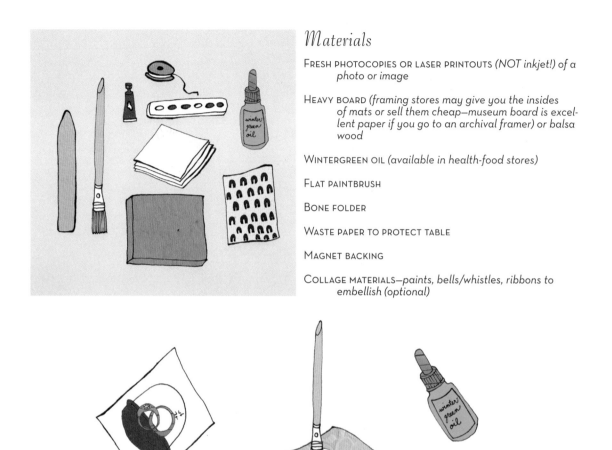

Materials

FRESH PHOTOCOPIES OR LASER PRINTOUTS *(NOT inkjet!) of a photo or image*

HEAVY BOARD *(framing stores may give you the insides of mats or sell them cheap—museum board is excellent paper if you go to an archival framer) or balsa wood*

WINTERGREEN OIL *(available in health-food stores)*

FLAT PAINTBRUSH

BONE FOLDER

WASTE PAPER TO PROTECT TABLE

MAGNET BACKING

COLLAGE MATERIALS—*paints, bells/whistles, ribbons to embellish (optional)*

1 Make a black-on-white photocopy or laser-print of a photo or image that you like. Cut balsa wood or mat board to size.

2 Lay the photocopy paper on the board and lightly paint the unprinted side of the photocopy with wintergreen oil.

3 Rub with a bone folder. This takes some practice—and the resulting texture is a little vague—try it and see if you like it.

4 Let it dry overnight. The smell of the wintergreen oil is intense—work in a place with good ventilation. (This can be tough in a city apartment.)

5 You can hand-color this image. Experiment with different media—color pencils, watercolor, acrylic—you could even make extra photocopies and cut away the areas you want to paint to make stencils. Add collage elements or even glitter, or stick-on jewels. Fridge magnets don't have to be tasteful! When you are happy with your result, attach the magnet backing.

NOTE: There are other photocopy-transfer methods. Most involve toxic solvents like acetone. Please be very aware of the danger of your materials. Don't do something for you wedding that keeps you from dancing at your twenty-fifth anniversary party.

Interlocking Announcement

I found inspiration for this interlocking card at the Metropolitan Museum's print study room in a stationer's order book of hideous 1950s wedding invitations. You need to cut the announcement out and score it before you fold so that the pieces interlock (all loving and romantic). Look at all kinds of things for format/structure ideas—you can figure out how to make it look good once you've figured out how it works.

Materials

TEMPLATE *(page 132)*

FOLDABLE, COVER-WEIGHT PAPER *big enough to allow for the template*

SCISSORS OR X-ACTO KNIFE

BONE FOLDER

⌒ **Liz Zanis made this engagement announcement.**

1 Start by making one for practice—a mock-up, or "dummy." Trace the template (page 132) on cover-weight paper, cut carefully, score with your bone folder, gently fold, and interlock—isn't it cool!

Once you get the hang of it, you could try variations of your own design—just be sure to use cheap or scrap paper to start with before you use the good stuff.

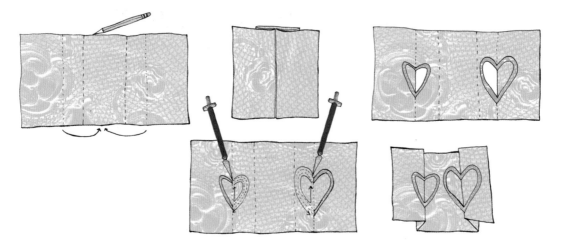

2 Plan your words, typesetting or handwriting, and print onto your cover-weight paper. You could handwrite them for a small quantity. Or make an original black-and-white photocopy, or scan it, and print onto paper before you cut it out.

Or print onto contrasting card stock. You could print several copies on a single page, and cut them. Attach to your cut-out card—with photo corners or slots that you cut or double-stick tape or glue—put a bit of tape or glue in the center of your cut-out card and float the contrasting card that has the words.

3 Once you've got a design you like, trace and cut your pattern.

4 Fold and insert into the envelopes.

Your save-the-date experience will let you know how involved you want to be with your actual invitation. Was this task enough for you, or are you raring to go further? Maybe, like me, you'll find yourself working on other people's weddings when you are done with your own.

Purgatory Pie Press handmade envelopes (opposite and pages 34–35). }

Make Your Own Envelopes

Materials

FOLDABLE PAPER

SCISSORS

ADHESIVE

If you'd like to make a save-the-date that doesn't fit a standard envelope or use paper that doesn't come pre-made as envelopes, it is easy to make your own. There are several ways to do this.

Making an envelope is like wrapping a package. Commercially made envelopes are designed for efficient large production. You can base your design on one of those, taking it apart and using it as a pattern, but you don't have to. I just figure out something that fits well and design an interesting shape. And then make my own template.

Make some trials from scrap paper, and then when you are happy with the shape and fit, make a pattern and trace it onto your good paper. Wrap the piece you want to send lightly in scrap paper, open the paper, and look at your creases. Envelopes need a top, bottom, and side flaps. As long as your envelope closes completely, you have much leeway on which flaps are bigger. Would you like pointed flaps or flat flaps, or do you want to cut them in a curve?

Here is an interesting trick for figuring out how much paper you need for square or squarish rectangle envelopes.

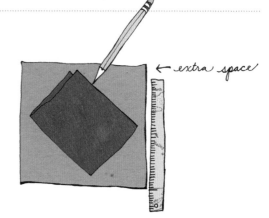

← extra space

1 Measure your invitation diagonally. Add a bit of "seam allowance"—overlap for glue—1/4" (6 mm) or so.

2 Measure and cut that square from some scrap paper and lay your invitation diagonally across it.

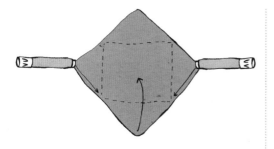

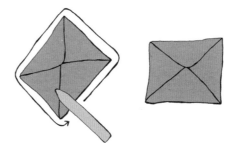

3 Fold in the sides, fold up the bottom, and fold down the top.

4 Look at the shape—do you like it? Trim here and there to make the shape more pleasing. Then flatten the envelope and trace the shape onto stiff paper to make your template.

5 Use this pattern to trace the shape onto your good paper. Cut it out, refold your template envelope, and fold your good paper around the template. You can address now or later. Glue the sides and bottom flap. Insert invitations and seal with glue or double-stick tape. Burnish.

NOTE: Paper with a pattern printed on one side can be nice for handmade envelopes—then you have an instant lining.

Send yourself one in the mail to test your paper before you go into production.

I made envelopes for our wedding invitations based on a 1920s envelope that I found in an antiques store. Wish I could find a sample to show you. I can at least give you a template for it in the back of this book (page 133) and show you my envelope. The original was all curves and swirls and lined with a beautifully silk-screened art-deco-patterned paper.

That envelope was hard to figure out, but I learned so much by doing it. Making them and lining them was my first experience in book-binding-style production. Whatever you need to do, break it down into steps and make a system. There is something pleasant and comforting about a pile of unfinished pieces becoming a pile of finished pieces.

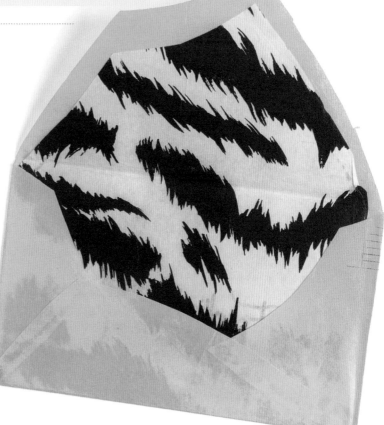

Envelope Linings

Purgatory Pie Press lined envelope and invitation.

If you are using store-bought envelopes, you can line them to make them more interesting. An envelope lining covers the inside of the flap and goes down below the opening of the envelope interior. To line a store-bought envelope, it's easiest to sacrifice one envelope to make a pattern for the rest, if they aren't too expensive. Or find a clean piece of paper for the pattern—reuse something for this—but if it's newspaper, make sure the printing won't rub off.

I was pricing an elaborate job once and visited an engraver who showed me a quick, easy way to make a liner pattern using an envelope.

Materials

FOLDABLE PAPER

SCISSORS

ADHESIVE

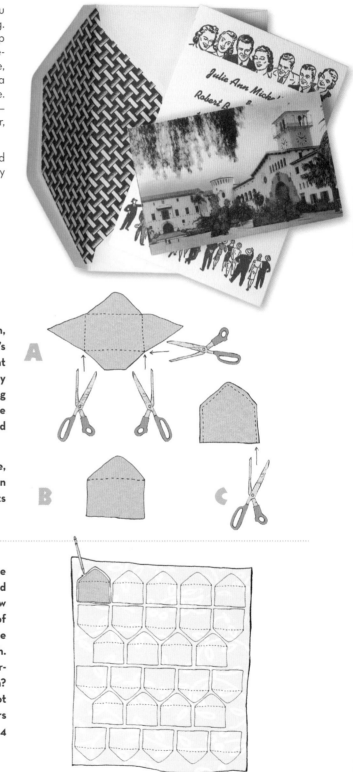

1 To sacrifice an envelope to make the pattern, gently pull or cut the envelope apart where it's glued. Trim the back plus a flap piece so that the glue strip will be exposed. This shape may look like a kid's drawing of a house (depending on your flap design). Trim the sides so that the liner is a little smaller than the envelope and will easily fit inside.

If your envelopes are too precious to sacrifice, trace an open envelope onto your pattern paper and then trim the pattern until it fits nicely inside.

2 Decide what interesting paper you'd like to use for lining. It needs to be fairly thin and fold easily. Make a little diagram to figure out how many liners you can make from one sheet of paper. Measure the height and width of the envelope at its widest points and do the math. Does the pattern need to fit on the paper in a certain way or can it go in more than one direction? I usually get one extra sheet of paper if it's not too expensive—but if your count has 20 liners per sheet and you need one more sheet for 44 pieces, you'll have plenty of extra already.

3 Once you have made your pattern, cut one sample from your decorative paper. Slide it into the envelope—does it slide in easily and look good? If so, shut the envelope to crease the liner. Place a piece of clean waste paper between the envelope and the flap. Open the flap so that the lining folds down over the waste paper. Glue the edges of the lining flap. Remove the waste paper, close the flap over the lining, and burnish well.

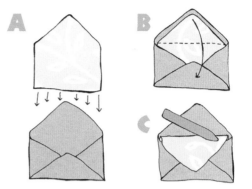

4 Check your lined envelope carefully—does it look good and function? Is your envelope flap glue still exposed? If you need to, make adjustments in your pattern and try another sample. If you are happy with it—go into production.

5 Trace your pattern onto your decorative paper as many times as you need it. You could start by making several patterns in case one wears out—you could even make a pattern from cardboard if you are doing quite a few.

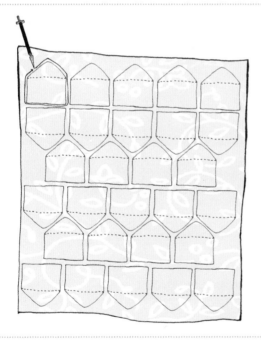

6 Cut out all your linings. Depending on their shape, you could use a paper chopper or scissors or a knife. I like to use sharp scissors, but some people prefer X-Acto knives—make sure your blade is very sharp, change blades often, and cut on a self-healing rubber mat. If you use a knife, you may want to make patterns from heavy cardboard, or set up a system so that you can cut against a metal-edged ruler or straight-edge. You may be able to set it up so that you cut long strips and then go back and trim the flap shape. If the lining paper is thin enough, you may be able to pile it up and cut a few at a time.

7 When you have all your linings cut, insert them into your envelopes and fold down the flap, creasing the lining.

8 Lay a clean waste sheet between the lining and the outside of the envelope (as shown). Glue around the flap edges with a glue stick or a fine line of glue from a squeeze bottle, or a thin coat of paste and a brush. Fold down the flap and burnish with a bone folder. Work slowly at first, but once you get the hang of it, these can go quickly.

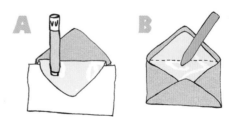

WILL ___ ATTEND

PLEASE RESPOND BY APRIL 30

THE PLEASURE OF YOUR COMPANY

Chapter 2
Invitation

Υ our invitation gives people a lot of information about your wedding.

It shows your style. It shows your taste. And hopefully people who see your sleek, spare, modern invitation won't send you ornate porcelain-gilded candlesticks with fat cupids—or vice versa. Though in our case, the invitation didn't seem to send that message—people just gave us "wedding gifts." We didn't register. Interesting weddings had not become part of the culture then. But now you can register at great places. And grabby as it may seem—do it. Include some inexpensive things. You don't want an absurd gift list to upstage the bride.

As you decide what you will do for your invitation, think about your wedding. How formal is it? How traditional do you want it to be? What are your traditions? Think about your budget. And time. (Are you richer in time or money?) Will you need to hire a calligrapher, or can you address your envelopes yourselves? (See the Handwriting Guide on page 130.) Maybe you can run envelopes through a computer printer. Inkjet printers are good for printing on all kinds of paper—and then you could match the type and color to your invitation. Can a friend do it for you? If it's a very small wedding, it's possible to handwrite each invitation.

For a larger guest list, you can type something simple on the computer and print it out onto nice paper or even on invitation blanks from office-supply stores. A high-quality photocopier can also work. Laser printers and photocopy machines take smooth paper best—and even if you can get them to print on textured papers, they may balk at quantity (I once had a Kinko's use up all their cream resume paper, trying to get solids to print without streaking). Inkjet printers work better with interesting papers. Test everything before you go too far. Start the process early and try things before you even design.

{ **Purgatory Pie Press invitation, hand-set metal type.**

A Word About Printing

But say you would like to have things printed. You need to know something about professional printing—and it's always changing.

Letterpress is what we do at Purgatory Pie Press, and of course we do it because we think it's the best—the type and image impress the paper, denting into it—We are true Luddites who prefer to hand-set antique wood and metal type—which most people think is ridiculously slow. Most letterpress printers design on the computer, make a film-negative output, and then make a polymer plate. Much quicker—except you have the expense of the negative output—and the turnaround time—with that AND the plate—and then when you are finished you throw away both plate and neg. By the time you've gone to all that trouble, you could have set your type—and when you are finished printing you sort the type back into the type case and can use it again for another project—waste not want not! (Though I always wait a few weeks to be safe, JUST IN CASE they need a few more—remember add 10 percent to everything for the just-in-cases.)

And here is the crazy thing. As I've been asking people about wedding invitations they have made—quite a few learned to do letterpress printing and typesetting for their wedding or their sister's or their best friend's wedding. It's not as hard or inaccessible as you'd think.

Dikko and I will have to write a book on letterpress printing soon—but for now, know that you could learn to do it if you wanted to—there are classes here and there—more and more as it's getting popular.

WITH PLEASURE

WITH REGRET

Silkscreen is another technique that many people use to print their own invitations. It often doesn't work as well for type—but some people can get excellent results. Silkscreen is something like stenciling. Same basic principle. You block out your negative space and print the positive, forcing ink through stretched-thin fabric onto your paper. There are services that will put your image onto a screen and sell you the ink and squeegee. My teenage daughter decided to silkscreen bags and T-shirts, and a friend advised her to take a black-and-white drawing and go to a store for everything she needed. This was just before I started teaching a course on artist books in a silkscreen room at the School for Visual Arts in New York. She could have gotten support and everything she needed there, so I was surprised that she went to a friend for help. But she managed to do it herself. She already had printmaking experience with linoleum cutting, but she found silkscreen easier.

Offset printing, also called litho, is what many people think of as "traditional printing." I think that's hilarious. Letterpress began with Gutenberg in the 1440s. Offset was a twentieth-century printing innovation, and it was not commonly used for high-quality printing until the 1960s. *Conventional printing* is a better term for it. It's how the book you are reading is printed. And for quantities of 2,000-plus it really makes sense. A good offset printer can do a beautiful job. But the press setup is very time-consuming. For small quantities it is not cost-effective. And good as it can be, when it's bad, it's horrid. Well, you can say that about most things, I guess. The best thing to print with offset is photography. I'm amazed that current magazines and mail-order catalogues have gorgeous photo printing that's much nicer than the plates used in expensive art books from the mid–twentieth century and before.

Engraving is considered the traditional way to print stationery. It's used for the formal invitations that people get from Tiffany's. Engraving is embossed, raised lettering, the opposite of letterpress' impression. You can tell if a card has been engraved, not thermographed (a method where plastic powder is heat-set onto printed type to make a raised effect) by checking the way it catches the light (the plastic in thermography is reflective)—and by feeling the back of the paper. If it's engraving, it indents a bit. Engraving plates used to be made by hand, but lately those, too, are computer originals. The old plates are very nice—but hand-engraving is one of the many dying arts/crafts. So if you go for engraving (and it is not something I can teach you in *The Paper Bride*) ask if the technicians are making the plates by hand. If they are not, it's not so traditional after all! But if they are using computer originals, you may be able to have more input, if that's what you want. The old plates were made with a very limited choice of typefaces—and the hand engravers traced these onto copper plates. If you do go to an engraver, ask if they'll take you on a tour to see the whole process. I think it's fascinating—but I love old machines—you may prefer the showroom. Nancy Sharon Collins, Stationer works with real traditional engraving. John Mack Collins took this photo.

Commercial digital printing has been taking the place of offset for many uses lately. It's cheaper for small quantities. Digital printing is changing so fast that as I write this paragraph a new press or new ink is probably being manufactured—but it's worth looking at. I have had antique postcards reproduced this way and then letterpress printed on the backs of them—I'm no purist!

And you may have your own excellent digital printer or access to a good one.

Inkjet and laser printers and photocopy machines may be sufficient for everything you need to make. You have to decide whether it's more frustrating to experiment on your own—there is always a trial-and-error aspect—or whether you'd rather work with a professional printer; then communication is the tricky part. Collaboration works for me. I love having people who are good at what they do contribute to a project. But many people prefer to do it themselves. There was some ad in the 1960s with a young woman saying, "Mother, I'd rather do it myself"—I can't remember what that was selling (tranquilizers were not advertised in those days—it was probably something for iron-poor blood). But some people work better alone—and you probably know if you are one of them. Throughout this whole process, listen to yourself. And if you are working with a vendor who tries to push you into something you don't want, change vendors. I just heard that one of my brides chose the comfortable wedding dress instead of the one that everyone else thought looked good—much to everyone else's chagrin. The one that looks good should be fitted so that it's comfortable—and it's not unreasonable to expect that.

↬ **Purgatory Pie Press invitation in the form of a giant matchbook, with postcard reply.**
Hand-set wood and metal type, hand-stitched.

A Word About Type

Typography is a huge subject (another book I'll have to write with Dikko!). What you call "fonts" we call typefaces—what can I say briefly? You need to look at things and see what you like. Rule of thumb is fewer typefaces combined look better than more. It's a rule we sometimes break—but you should have a good reason for breaking it. We shy away from typical wedding script faces, and I usually don't like italics—but the type we chose for this book (the one you are reading!) is an example of a type with an italic that I do like—I tend to like type pretty small on the page with a lot of negative space.

Also, assuming you may be designing on the computer—be sure to print things out and look at them; often people design on the screen and don't see how it looks printed. My last book had an issue where one page was somehow reduced—and because a trimmed copy was never checked, the discrepancy wasn't caught. You don't want to waste resources, but proofing is never a waste—it's like tasting your caterer's food—even if they charge for that, you must do it. I went to a wedding where the food looked pretty, but was dried out and tasteless. You don't want people to remember your wedding for the dry chicken.

Since computer design has become standard, many people design things like business cards large, and then when they are printed, see them small for the first time. Think about who will be reading your invitation. Tiny gray type on pale green paper is hard for anyone over thirty-five to read. Who is your audience? Make something that they can see—without compromising your taste. The less color contrast, the bigger the type should be. Some people do two versions of their save-the-dates—one for friends and another for family members. If you are making your own wedding invitations, you could do the same thing—just running different-color papers through your printer or photocopier could give you very different looks. But you could customize more than that—making something that won't upset your relatives and something very different that your friends will appreciate.

So what can I tell you about type? Look at things—collect bits and pieces. Did I tell you I found the typeface for this book on a menu? I asked the waiter if I could buy a copy, and luckily they had a take-out version. We researched it and figured out what it was. But start really looking at printed ephemera—at other people's invitations, but also business cards, ads in magazines—old things that you find at yard sales and flea markets. These are the things to start collecting in the envelopes of that paper pocket planner you made (page 16).

LA HABANA CUBA
NATALIE COE y EDUARDO LLANOS
10 JUNIO 95
RSVP: SRC

JANET L. RUMBLE
MATT LITTLEJOHN
28 MINETTA LANE, N-20
NEW YORK CITY 10012

TOGETHER WITH THEIR FAMILIES

. RUMBLE
&
. LITTLEJOHN

URE OF YOUR COMPANY

WEDDING

URDAY
OF SEPTEMBER
ELEVEN O'CLOCK
MORNING

FONTE HOTEL
SEWELL STREETS
NEW JERSEY

N TO FOLLOW

A POSTCARD

The Way to Cape May

Cape May is on the southern-most tip of the New Jersey shore.

From Atlantic City (48 miles):
Atlantic City Expressway West to the Garden State Parkway South to Route 109 South.

From Philadelphia (87 miles): Walt Whitman Bridge to Route 42 South to the Atlantic City Expressway East to the Garden State Parkway South to Route 109 South.

From New York City (169 miles): Interstate 95 (the New Jersey Turnpike) South to the Garden State Parkway South to Route 109 South.

The Chalfonte is in the heart of Victorian Cape May's historic district. After crossing the Canal and Marina bridges, proceed to the first traffic light. Turn left at the light onto Madison Avenue. After the water tower, make your second right onto Sewell Street. The hotel is located on the corner of Howard and Sewell streets.

To Stay in Cape May

The Chalfonte Hotel (609) 884-8409
The Hotel Macomber (609) 884-3020
For help with bed & breakfast accommodations, please call Kathy Keller at the Cape May Reservation Service (800) 729-7778

Beach & Boardwalk and Ocean Front Cottages at Cool Cape May, N. J.

Leslie Marcus & Aytan Diamond
invite you to join them to
celebrate their wedding

Saturday, October 18, 1997
6:30 pm Ceremony

Dinner & Dancing
to follow

Angel Orensanz
Foundation
172 Norfolk Street
New York City

Mr. and Mrs. Arthur Bierwirth, Jr.
request the pleasure of your company
at the marriage of their daughter

fer Lynn
to

Craig Shurman

leventh of November
thousand
the evening

iculture Center
a, Pennsylvania

The Favour of a Reply is Requested by the Eleventh of October

Reception to follow   Black Tie Optional

⌐ **Purgatory Pie Press invitations, printed from hand-set metal type.**

Writing the Words for Your Invitation

The words are the first thing you need for your invitation (well, that and the paper stock, size, color, typeface—but really the words are a good place to start).

You will find lots of conflicting info on the Web about what to say. Watch your sources—and this is one of those times to decide on your tradition and level of formality and pretentiousness. How do you feel about *honor* and *honour*? Do you or your fiancé have a Dutch middle name? (If you do, be sure you know how to spell it before you print the invitations.)

Are you mentioning parents? Bride's parents only? Or bride's and groom's? Miss Manners says this is not a bill of lading. But still, if parents are paying for the wedding, they may want to be the official hosts. If your parents are married to other people, it gets complicated—"together with their families" is how many people handle that. I don't like "together with"—it sounds awkward—but then again awkwardness is probably one of the charms of a wedding.

Mr. and Dr. Brett Goldstein
Request the Honor of Your Presence
at the wedding of their daughter
Jamie Brett
to
Ryan Kinney
Saturday September twenty-second
at five in the evening
at
The Village Synagogue
12th Street
New York City

STACY AND JAMIE BRILL
REQUEST THE PLEASURE OF YOUR
COMPANY
AT THE
WEDDING RECEPTION
OF

LILY & IAN
SATURDAY, SEPTEMBER 30TH
AT
BOULEY
HUDSON & DUANE STREETS
NEW YORK CITY
COCKTAILS AT 7
DINNER AT 8
DANCING TO FOLLOW

THE FAVOR OF A REPLY IS REQUESTED BY SEPTEMBER 2

Ashley Jordan & Jordan Ashley
request the pleasure of your company
at their wedding

Sunday, June 13
at 3 in the afternoon
in the
Cobble Hill Garden
Clinton St & Verandah Place
Brooklyn

Dinner and dancing to follow

THEO DARLING & MICK HOLLYWOOD
INVITE YOU TO THEIR WEDDING
OCTOBER 30, 5 PM
AT THE
SARGENT MANSION
IN
STATEN ISLAND
WEAR YOUR DANCING SHOES!

The Honor of Your Presence is American tradition if you are having a religious ceremony in a place of worship. For a church wedding, the reception is often in a separate location and so may have an separate invitation—usually sent in the same envelope. I always warn people about sending out invitations at times when they will end up in a pile of mail—say, in August, when many people are away on vacation—or in December, when they could get lost in a pile of holiday cards. If your wedding is in a secular location—even if clergy is officiating—the formal wording is "the Pleasure of Your Company."

I always recommend that you tell people on the invitation if they will be eating. Since there are many versions of what used to be called "mixed" marriages now, people have different traditions and different expectations.

Jewish and Italian weddings include feasts. Chinese weddings have banquets—but some weddings are more liquor based and sometimes only include a few passed hors d'oeuvres. People need to know whether to come hungry or after a good meal. Especially if they will be traveling on the wedding day.

Try to be clear about what people need to wear for comfort. If the terrain will not support spike heels, better to know ahead of time. What's difficult, what's awkward—and what's wonderful about weddings is the great range in ages of the attendees—so think about your oldest and youngest guests. You don't need to get ridiculously specific in the invitation, but you may want to informally warn people if you think they will be uncomfortable.

There are many other ways to write your words. Look at traditions from other countries—check etiquette books from other eras. Or make up anything that works for you.

Just be careful about phrases like "share in our joy"—I think *sharing* should go back to meaning sharing toys and candy (which you may remember isn't much fun!). And *joy*—joy is assumed in a wedding—you don't have to spell it out.

I love to use the word *celebrate*—but in Episcopal weddings, that has another meaning and is the domain of the priest or "celebrant."

Celebrate
the wedding
of

Ashley
&
Jordan

Sunday, May 31
at 3 pm
Venice Beach
California

feast & festivities
follow

flip-flops optional

Jim and Debbie Zug

cordially invite you to the

rehearsal dinner for

Rebecca Loud & Jim Zug

Bring your laughter, love and song to a summer

barbecue

for all our friends and family
Friday 22 June 2001 starting at six in the evening
Codman Community Farm, Lincoln, Massachussetts

There are moments when the body is as num
as words, days be ore the good flesh cor
Such tendern moons and
saying ble

Rowing in Ea
Ah, the Sea
Might I but moo
in Thee

Emily Dickinson

Gertrude Stein

nk I do love all
Love love all you wi
d bless my baby

1761   A HARLEQUIN ROMANCE   60¢

STARS THROUGH THE MIST

Special
Wedding
Edition

Betty Neels

r his shoulder,
BLAIR MARK &
ADAM CASDIN
eart. This pi
ire.
re s

January 17,

Betsy Dunham Blachly **&** Henry Chapin
are happy to announce
their marriage celebration
February 18th 1989
St **A**mbrose Chapel
Cathedral of St John the Divine
W.
lunched at The Symposium
jumped the broom
& went skiing with our children
Margaret, Simeon, Willa & Jamie

Same as ever
Hallelujah

Pinewoods Camp

Long Pond

Plymouth Massachusetts

Give me a boat that will carry two

Dick & Dixie Peaslee
request the honor of your presence
at the wedding of

Jessica Dixon Peaslee
&
Wilfrid Eliseo Zogbaum

Ben Hartley and Christine Schwartz are **Married**

Paris 1995

NewYork September 24, 1994

Sydney January, 1995

World

RSVP

{ Purgatory Pie Press invitations, printed from hand-set metal and wood type.

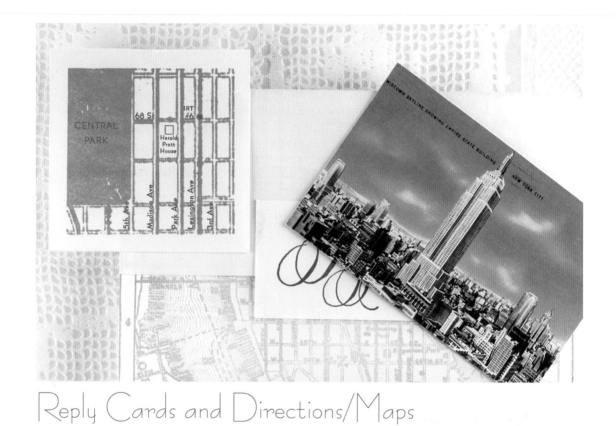

Reply Cards and Directions/Maps

I recommend reply dates early enough so that people reply as soon as they get the invitations instead of putting them aside—so if it needs to be at the beginning of a month, do it at the end of the month before—August 31 seems so much sooner than September 1.

And speaking of RSVP cards, the current standard seems to be

M_____

will __attend.

sometimes with choices of food, so the caterer knows how much of what to prepare.

O grilled salmon

O filet mignon

O vegetarian

O vegan

O dairy free

O allergic to _____

⌐ **Purgatory Pie Press invitations.**
Opposite—printing plates made from lace from the bride's dress, custom handmade paper.   }

Right before the 2008 election, we were working on an invitation with a voting component—guests got to vote for cake flavors (I need a snack as I write this)—vanilla, yellow, chocolate, marble. And icings—chocolate or vanilla. And fillings—chocolate pudding, mousse, whipped cream, custard—

People are irresponsible. Have you ever lost an RSVP card under a pile of more urgent papers? So it's up to you to come up with some fail-safes. And order 10 percent extra of everything just in case. You don't want to offend someone by serving them on a silver plate when everyone else gets gold! They might put a curse on your child and have her prick her finger with a spindle.

You can very lightly number the cards corresponding to your list so that if you receive one without a name or in illegible handwriting, you can figure out whose it is—and also so that you can call the people who haven't responded. One set of parents misunderstood this stealth idea and wrote big bold numbers in thick black marker. It made me sad to think of our beautiful RSVP cards being desecrated like that. It also created much confusion among the guests—and on some level it became an in-joke that was part of the fun. That's the thing about weddings—stuff goes wrong and that's part of what makes them interesting and memorable. Think of your current frustration as future good stories—"When mommy and daddy got married . . ."

Formal Invitations, with Envelope

You can, of course, include a self-addressed stamped envelope and a matching card. It may seem more formal, or more "traditional"—though traditions vary—and really the proper etiquette would be to expect guests to be well bred enough to use their own initial note cards and write a formal response:

> *Jule Thomas is pleased to accept the invitation to your wedding*
> *as well as the reception following on June 22nd.*

Another envelope is another design element—it can be a smaller version of the invitation envelope or you can choose contrasting colors or an interesting shape. The card can be a single sheet or folded—and like the postcard version can have preprinted prompts or just a line requesting a reply.

Postcard Reply

You can use postcards as reply cards instead of cards in envelopes. It makes a flatter invitation package and saves some paper and even some printing. Even if it gets a dinged in the mail, it will look pristine when your guests first see it.

Postcard responses can be as elegant or as interesting as you like. The simplest match the wedding invitation—same paper, same color. You can either put your address on one side and the reply on the other, or have an image on one side, like a regular postcard, and split the back with your address and stamp on the left and the reply portion on the right.

If you'd like people to write personal notes—something that can be fun to look back on over the years—or even incorporated into your album—leave a blank space with instructions—"RSVP by December 15"—or "Kindly reply by March 11" or "The Favor of Your Reply is Requested."

If you put those words at the bottom left, it may prevent people from writing too close to the bottom where the post office is likely to place a bar-code sticker.

The postcard, no matter what wording you'd like to use, can be whatever style most appeals to you. Some people even get a whole collection of different postcards, knowing they will get them back with personal notes as a wedding keepsake. If you are using vintage postcards, check to be sure they are big enough to go through the mail—the sizes change from time to time, so make sure to check. If the size is too small, you could scan, enlarge, and print them out on card stock. I usually make a test or two and send one to myself to make sure they go through the mail. Once I opened my mailbox to find a beautiful postcard, and after a few minutes realized that I had sent it to myself as a test—I thought it was a genuine antique card, instead of a reproduction.

You may find postcards that go with the theme of your wedding in some way—say, relating to location—or art museum reproductions that have special meaning.

⌒ **Purgatory Pie Press RSVP with a woodcut by the groom Wil Zogbaum. Our leverage operated guillotine saved the day when we were able to trim their invitations even though we had no electricity in September 2001.**

clockwise from upper left: Invitations by Lissi Erwin, Jon Snyder, Phil Zimmerman, Laura Reddick and Daniel Roode, Josh Levi, Deb Wood and Dave Konopka, and Joshua Schreier (center).

Message-in-a-Bottle

If you can never throw away a soda bottle with cool typography, this a wonderful way to use them. They could also be shower invitations or invitations to an anniversary party (is there a glass anniversary?) or thank-you notes—or as a low-tech alternative to blogging.

Materials

BOTTLES

BOTTLE BRUSH *(optional)*

PAPER—*something fun and lightweight that will go through your photocopier or printer*

STRING OR RIBBON *(optional)*

CAPS OR CORKS *(optional)*

1 Collect your bottles. This project makes sense for a smaller wedding. I love Mexican soda bottles. My favorite hole-in-the-wall taco place (they also have pizza by the slice, but the authentic Mexican food is amazing) has boxes for the empties. Work something out with your favorite local taco stand. Or have a huge party (one of the showers?) and keep the empties. Clean and dry them. A bottle brush could help!

2 See what paper size makes sense for your bottles. You will be rolling it to fit inside. Either horizontal or vertical is fine. Use a standard paper size that will go in your printer or photocopy machine, but you can trim it to make it more interesting.

3 Put the words on your original. If you are photocopying, keep the original black on white, even if you will be using color or textured paper. Handwriting this makes sense—what you'd really find in a message in a bottle. But do anything you like for the type—use an old typewriter or do something on a computer.

4 Print (via photocopy or computer printer, or whatever you'd like—letterpress if you have it!) and trim your paper. Roll it and tie with a string or ribbon and place it in the bottle. Cork or cap it if you like.

5 Mailing these could be tricky—and I can't recommend throwing them into the ocean if your wedding is anytime soon. I googled "boxes" and found many choices. Pack them carefully. Shred wedding magazines for packing material. Or find something else fun to pack with—like roasted peanuts or air-popped corn. One mail-order spice seller packs in cinnamon sticks! In January, look for a source for chipped Christmas trees. Our local park got a shipment for mulch and the smell is lovely.

6 Do something fun with the mailing labels. Look for interesting vintage labels. You can scan and print or photocopy the vintage ones onto sticky-back paper if you don't have enough.

Jessica Bauman
&
Benjamin Posel

together with
our families

invite you to

CELEBRATE

our wedding

Sunday at noon
June 21 1998

Sunny Oaks Hotel
Woodridge New York

BBQ
FESTIVITIES POOLSIDE
Saturday   June 20   6 pm

Pop-Up Invitation

This doesn't even pretend to be traditional—but it can be as elegant as you like, depending on your type and paper choices. Beautiful handwriting or simple, elegant type can be very nice for this. Remember to make your original black ink on white paper if you will be photocopying—but print on any color paper that you like. Print and test until you are happy before you make the whole bunch.

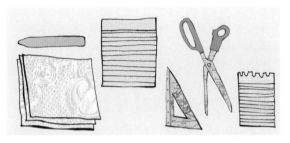

Materials

FOLDABLE, HEAVY-WEIGHT PAPER *that will feed through your printer*

BONE FOLDER

RULED PIECE OF PAPER

TRIANGLE

SCISSORS

1 Fold your paper in half and fold back the other way, reversing the fold and burnishing.

2 Use your bone folder to trace a half circle onto your paper. Cut an odd number of slits, at least five or seven. Fold alternating strips—folding the first and last strips. Unfold, turn your paper over, and refold on the other side to reverse the creases. Unfold again.

3 Use the triangle to draw straight lines, from the marks on the fold to the edge of the circle. Cut these lines and fold out along the edge, alternating strips—folding the first and last strips. Unfold, turn your paper over, and refold on the other side to reverse the creases. Unfold again.

4 Form paper into a tent, using one hand for support, and pop the folded strips toward the inside. Close the tent, burnish, and then gently open and close to check the motion.

5 Experiment with paper and pop-up sizes until you are happy with the results. Then plan your words to fit on the strips. Design with enough space so that if things shift a little in printing, nothing will get chopped off.

We used a contrasting paper for the reply postcard and put that in the envelope behind the pop-up so that it showed through the slits.

{ Pop-up invitation by Purgatory Pie Press, hand-set type.

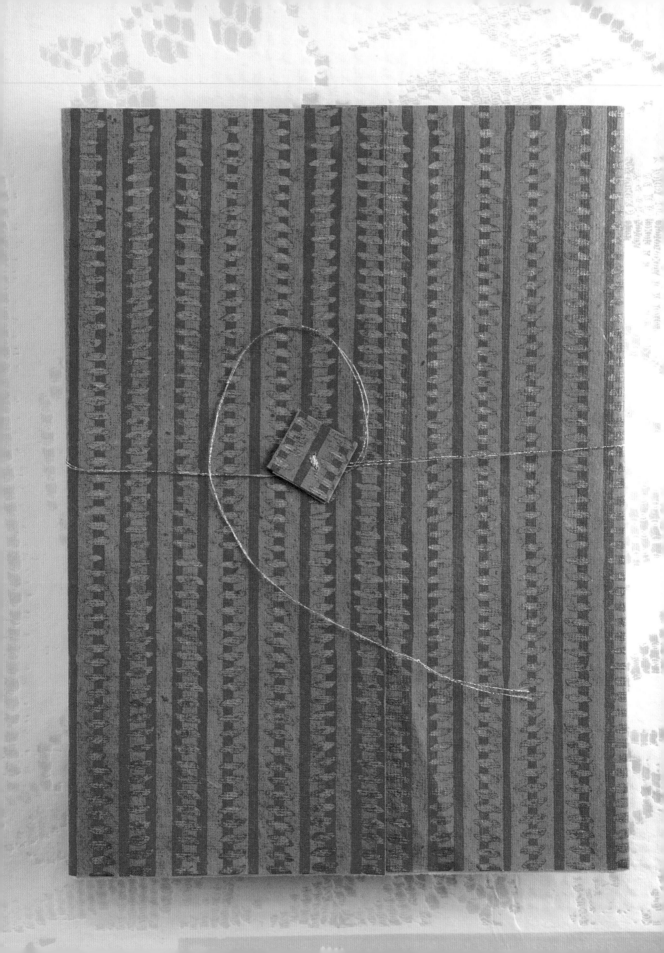

Wraps with Paper Buttons

There are some traditions that don't do much for me—the envelope in the envelope and the little tissue paper. The tissue was used with engraving, so that the ink wouldn't smear—it might make sense if you use engraving. The envelope inside the envelope just seems wasteful and pretentious (reminds me of those ladies who would wear white gloves and check to see if your windowsills are dusty). But there is something nice about a ceremonial opening for your invitation—and one way to do this is with a wrap. Another nice thing about a wrap is that it will pull focus away from the invitation—so if you've saved money by printing it yourself on nice paper via inkjet, people may be wowed enough by the wrap not to notice.

Your wrap can be made of any paper that appeals to you (and folds)—something lightweight and elegant and decorative. Think about the colors you'd like to use in your wedding—choosing this paper may even help you find colors that you will want to repeat in your flowers or on your table or in attendants' dresses.

You don't have to have a closure for your wrap. Just folding it so it overlaps could be enough. Or you could punch a few holes or cut some slits and weave a ribbon. One thing I like to do is make a paper button.

Materials

THIN, INTERESTING PAPER *(for wrap and for button)*

SCISSORS

BONE FOLDER

THREAD AND NEEDLE

GLUE *(optional)*

1 Cut your paper so that it is the same height as your invitation and more than twice as wide. Wrap the paper around your invitation so there is an overlap. It can overlap just a little, or as much as you like.

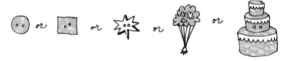

2 To make the button, choose a paper. It can be something thick, or you could take thin paper and fold it into itself and burnish. If you made your wrap from lightweight paper, you could use scraps for these buttons. No need to use adhesive, since sewing will keep it shut—but if a spot of glue makes it easier, it won't hurt.

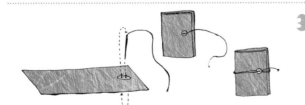

3 Sew it on like a button, either punching holes ahead of time or making them with your needle as you sew. Tie off your thread, but instead of cutting, leave it long enough to go around the wrap and wind around your button.

{ Purgatory Pie Press Invitation Wraps with Paper Buttons. Printing plates made from seashells and map collage. Hand-set metal type. ↶

Pop-Up Map

If you need to include a map or directions, think about how that will look as part of your stationery. It makes me sad when I see something ugly, badly stuffed into an invitation envelope. The map can be a beautiful element instead of a detriment. You may find an artist or a kid who likes to draw to create an interesting map—or find an interesting old one. The map can be printed simply on a card, the same size or a little smaller than the invitation—or it could even be printed on thin paper, folded nicely, and inserted. You could use the map as a folder for the invitation—an inner envelope replacement, but a useful one. This pop-up map is an effort but can be fun. (You can have a map-folding brunch—for precise friends only!) It makes this piece of information into an interesting or elegant keepsake.

Materials

LIGHTWEIGHT, LETTER-SIZE PAPER

BONE FOLDER

FOLDABLE, COVER-WEIGHT PAPER *(see page 27)*

ADHESIVE OF CHOICE

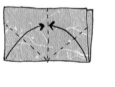

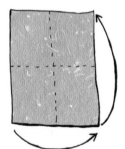

1 Fold a letter-size piece of paper in half vertically, open, then fold horizontally.

2 With the fold at the bottom, fold both bottom ends up to the center, and vertical-fold so that the folded edges meet and the bottom of the paper comes to a point. Burnish. Unfold and fold the opposite side on the same crease, reversing your fold. Burnish well.

{ Pop-up map drawn by Georgia Luna

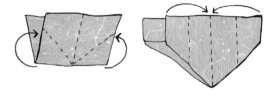

the popping of the pop up

3 Unfold back to that first horizontal, and tuck the folded corner inside. Just pinch one side, unfold the opposite corner, and tuck that corner fold into the center. It sort of pops in if you've burnished really well. Repeat this on the other side. It's the trickiest part of this map fold. Once you get it, the rest is easy.

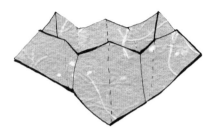

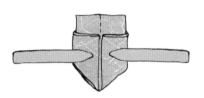

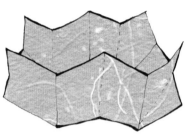

4 Now fold the short flat sides into the center of the paper, both on the front and the back, burnish, and reverse folds.

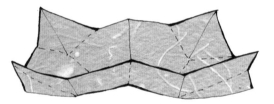

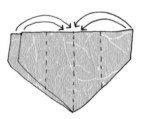

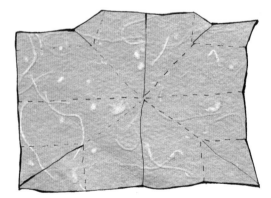

5 As you did before, tuck these folds inside—unfold one of the folds, put your forefinger inside, and push in with your thumb. Repeat with the other three folds and (as always!) burnish well.

6 Try opening and closing—it should pop open and refold.

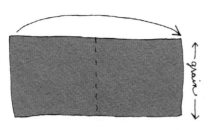

7 Check the cover-stock grain to be sure that you'll be folding it along the path of least resistance (see page 27). Cut your cover paper a little wider than your folded piece and at least twice as long. Fold it in half—don't make your fold too sharp—you will burnish it later.

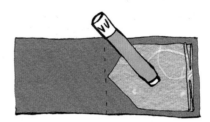

8 Now attach the map fold to the cover. To do this, place the map fold inside, with the point touching the fold of the cover.

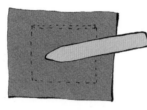

9 Apply adhesive to the interior paper, fold the cover up, and close it over the inner piece. Burnish the cover over the adhesive, protecting with a waste sheet so that the bone folder doesn't mark it.

10 Turn the piece over, open the other side, put adhesive on the inner folded paper, and close the cover on that side. This system of opening and closing the cover might seem odd, but it allows for the right amount of hinging space so that the map will open without ripping the paper. Try this a few times with junk paper until you get the hang of it.

You can use photocopies or printouts, but try a few before you commit. Sometimes toner will rub off if it's on the fold. Some papers hold the toner better than others.

To print on a black-and-white photocopier, use white paper for your original. Draw with black pens, soft pencils, or black markers. I hate the smell of Sharpies, so I use a water-based version. As long as you don't cry on it, it doesn't need to be waterproof.

What would you like for your map cover? It could be simple and informative like: Map to Erica and John's Wedding. Or a design with your initials: E&J. Or use a design element from your other wedding pieces. We made a map invitation: We printed the words on a map cover and had a map collaged from antique map sources inside—it wasn't meant to be informative, but it made the invitation into a beautiful keepsake.

Your cover-weight paper may feed through the photocopier. Or you can photocopy onto sticky-back paper to make a label. Or you can print onto lightweight paper, cut out your labels, and adhere. To make your own stickers, set up your originals to copy a bunch of labels at a time, back the whole sheet with a sheet of double-stick tape, then just cut up and adhere. This isn't worth the trouble for five or ten invitations, but if you are making twenty-five or more, it saves time and materials. It's also good to know this technique for future projects. This works well when you want to use color images but are being thrifty about your color copies. Crowd as many pictures as you can onto your original, color-copy it, and then chop it up and use it for a touch of color on cheaper copies.

It can be nice to add a little collage to each piece. Of course, this can be done on the computer if you know how. But, as artist Stephanie Brody-Lederman (who made the lanterns on page 100) reminds me, the mark of the hand can be most beautiful. Elements of rubber-stamping can be great, too, either stamped on an original and then photocopied, or done on each individual invitation. Practice stamping, and when you are comfortable with your technique, set yourself up to do the whole job.

Thank-You Notes and Stationery
(Let People Know Your Married Name)

It makes sense to plan your thank-you notes now, even though it seems early. I remember hearing something like you have a whole year after the wedding to send thank-you notes—but people like to get them sooner. Some people feel you should acknowledge the gift before the sun sets on the day you open the present. Depending on how much leisure time your guests have, ripping you to shreds for not sending thank-you notes fast enough could be a form of amusement for them. Thank-you notes also let people know your address and what names you will be using when you are married. Like everything else, there are many things called "traditional." Some people's tradition is to wait until prints come back from the photographer to enclose with the note. Others have stationery to use before they are married and then other stationery for after the wedding. Some people feel the stationery should only have the name of the person writing the note.

Macs for Dummies, when I first read it, had a hilarious approach to writing thank-you notes. It had you make a database with name, address, gift, and adjective. And then a Mad Libs–style form letter. Dear <u>Jimmy,</u> Thank you so much for the <u>Harley</u>. It was the most <u>expensive</u> gift I have ever received. Best, Debby. If you use this idea, try not to let anyone know.

I typed mine because we'd hand-rolled our thank-you notes with a large swath of ink that resisted the ink of the markers I liked using then. (Which was back in the typewriter days—jeez! I also had an office job with much downtime—so the click of my typewriter made me sound busy.) Ballpoint pens have recently become a favorite for me—maybe because the bank started giving them free (as I write this, not sure if that bank will collapse—I think a Canadian company absorbed it—will they keep giving free pens?)—or because MoMA featured a simple Bic ballpoint pen in an exhibit about information design a few years ago, and I began to appreciate them, but also ballpoint pens will write on coated papers.

So think about thank-you notes—will you write them on postcards from places you visit on your honeymoon?—hopefully you will not wish they were here! Or vintage postcards? Or stationery printed with your name or initials? A timely holiday card? Or use an image from your invitation or RSVP. We are making invitations for animal lovers right now. We found a really cute old metal engraving of a dog—we are printing that for the thank-you cards, too.

{ I collaged wedding photos, lace and fabric for these photocopy cards and printed on art papers.

Boys Allowed!

Chapter 3
Showers & Parties

*B*etween the engagement and the wedding,
you may have a few events.

It's yet another time when *traditional* can mean many things, depending on your traditions. Some people have women's parties (some people call them hen parties—apparently a popular term in England). Traditionally, the bride needed things to set up her own household—but you may already have a home with things—so being showered with gifts may not be such a necessity. But the tradition remains to celebrate. Plus you might want cool new stuff. Depending on the length of your engagement, you may or may not have time for a shower. Some people will have many with different crowds—even family size is a factor.

Like your wedding, showers can range in style and theme. One friend had a vintage kitchen-things shower—every gift had to come from a yard sale or thrift shop—I gave her an old painted tin-covered cake plate. Someone else gave her sheets of lovely antique gift wrap—she was a book artist, so paper was a perfect present.

{ We reuse magazine paper to clean our press and then it looks so interesting that I keep it to re-reuse. We made this table runner from it and Ashley Soliman made the paper doll's dress.

Shower Invitations

Shower invitations can be whatever style fits the shower—usually they are simpler than wedding invitations—but some showers are very formal. I went to one intimate tea with engraved invitations where the hostess told me the bride collected Waterford crystal. The centerpiece at the table was so big we had to lean around it to see each other. For others, an e-mail invitation is enough. Though, since this book is about paper, I can't encourage that. Depending on the number of people, you can have fun hand-making each one, handwriting each invitation. Handwrite on postcards—find a museum card with art that reminds you of the bride—or vintage postcards—color-photocopy onto card stock if necessary—though if you are doing that, set the invitations up to be two-sided and you can handwrite one and copy it onto the rest. Or print them with inkjet. And letterpress is becoming so accessible that you can find a printer easily or try doing it yourself. Silkscreen is also an excellent option. If you want to recycle, cut postcards from cereal boxes—those bright colors look interesting when you randomly cut them.

If the shower has an activity theme, you can enclose something in the envelope. Like a quilt square for each person to sign or embroider that can be pieced and quilted at the party. Or as in the cookbook project (page 70)—a recipe card.

⌐ **Jennifer King photocopied this accordion shower invitation from her handwritten text and drawings.**

Accordion Invitation

Jennifer King made this for her sister's wedding shower when she was first interested in book arts. She remembers working on them with one of the other bridesmaids—who later told her how difficult she thought the project had been—while Jen enjoyed all the handwork. Know before you bite off this project, that you may find it tedious if you don't love folding paper, etc.

Materials

LETTER SIZE "RESUME" PAPER

BONE FOLDER

NARROW SATIN RIBBON —*approximately 15" per book*

COVER-WEIGHT PAPER

PHOTOCOPIER *or* COMPUTER PRINTER

1. **Plan to print four or five of these, on a length of office paper. Start with some scrap paper to make a preliminary version to design/plan your accordion.**

   Take a strip of paper that's the full length of your paper and an inch or 2 (2.5–5 cm) wide. Accordion-fold to make six or more pages—you can plan that the pages will be approximately square—but if you prefer wider or narrower pages, fold those.

2. **Use this preliminary piece to design and plan your words and pictures, making a dummy. Sketch lightly and then handwrite and draw your information. You can use some clip art or photo booth photos, etc., for illustrations, or rubber stamps, stickers—**

3. **Make a final version in black ink on white paper. Flatten out this original and make three copies. (Or scan and set up on the computer.) Paste up and print as many copies as you need, dividing the number of guests by the number of accordions you can fit on your paper (so if you have 20 guests, divided by 4 per sheet, you need 5 sheets of paper—or maybe 6 for a few extras, just in case).**

4. **Make your covers by cutting the heavier paper a bit larger than the inside—with enough extra on the front to slit for the ribbon (see photo)—and attach to the outsides, one on either end—with double-stick tape.**

5. **Take narrow ribbon and thread it through the covers. Knot the ends so they won't pull out. Fold shut, pull the ribbon tight, wrap, and tie with a bow.**

This can be an invitation sent in an envelope (find one that you like or make your own from the instructions on page 34). Or use it as a favor. You could write a poem on it or a simple recipe.

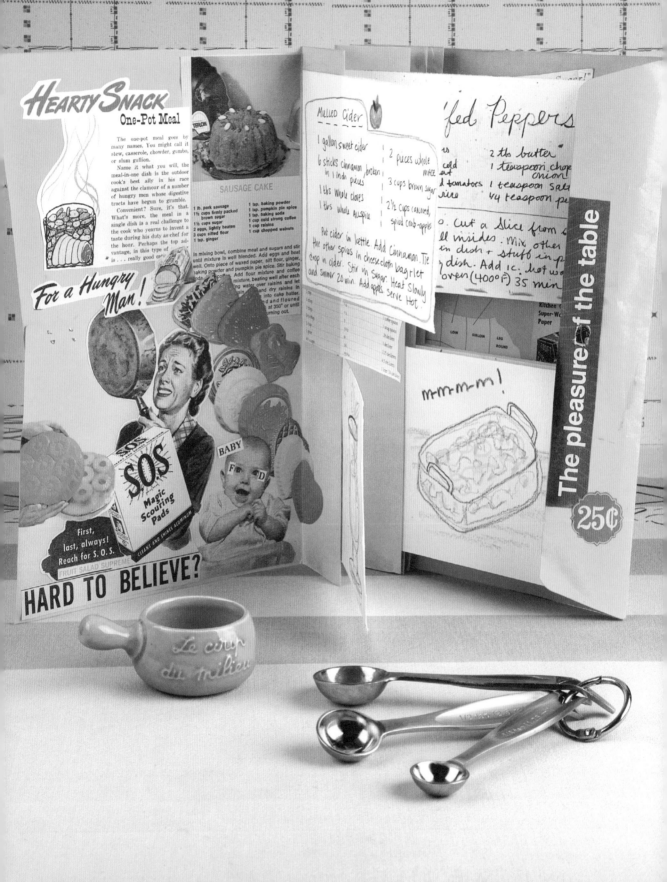

Flag Book Cookbook

Bookbinder Hedi Kyle invented this amazing and very easy structure in the 1970s for a Center for Book Arts exhibit at the Elaine Benson Gallery in South Hampton, Long Island. Gary Frost, a bookbinder/historian named it the flag book. I sometimes call it flip flap after its lively sound and action.

The cookbook potluck shower can be fun for people who cook—or people who can do creative things with the idea of recipes. A community cookbook we contributed to had a joke recipe for BBQ Elephant to serve 500—ingredients: 1 elephant, 200 gallons of BBQ sauce.

Your invitation might advise guests to cook their favorite secret family recipe for the potluck. They can bring the food in kitchen items that will serve as gifts. If the bride needs a set of dishes—particularly a set of vintage dishes—those could even be used for the potluck.

Include a card for the recipe when you send the invitation—and maybe extras in case someone makes a mistake. Tell guests to only write on one side, or make a clear margin so that they don't write where you will need to attach the card to the book. You can do this with a piece of peel 'n' stick double-stick tape.

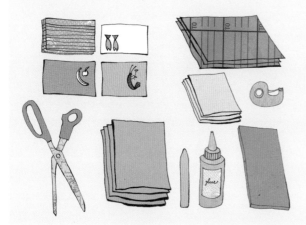

Materials

RECIPE CARDS—*use index cards or cut your own from card stock*

HEAVY, FOLDABLE PAPER

COVER—*raw book-binding board or museum board, or recycle old book covers, boxes, etc.*

DOUBLE-STICK TAPE *or* BOOKBINDING PASTE *or* GLUE

BONE FOLDER

SCISSORS

DECORATIVE END PAPERS *(optional)*

WASTE SHEETS

1 Think about how many cards you will be including in this book before you begin—try making a quick dummy book from scrap paper to learn the form and try out some sizes and ideas (I explain more about dummy books on page 77). Your book will need an extra fold in the front and one in the back to attach to the cover.

2 Fold a narrow accordion from heavy, foldable paper. Make it tall enough to accommodate two to three recipe cards.

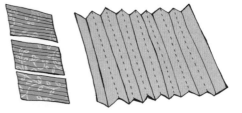

3 Make covers from plain board, or cover the board with book cloth or paper (instructions on page 19). If you are recycling, a cut-up box can continue the theme. Cut your cover boards big enough to accommodate the height of the narrow accordion plus the width of your cards (once they are attached).

{ Ashley Soliman made this flagbook—Lissi added the recipe cards.

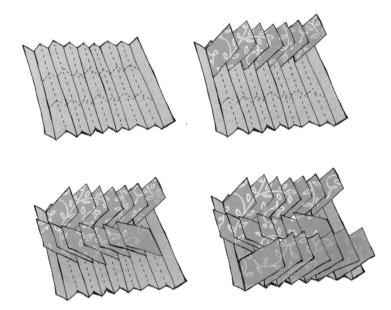

4 Lay out your finished recipe cards on the accordion so that they look interesting and don't bump when opened, alternating sides of the accordion and glue as shown.

5 Glue the accordion to the covers, burnishing well (as always!).

6 Cut decorative end sheets a bit smaller than the covered board and glue to hide bare board and raw edges of cloth.

7 Weight carefully and let dry overnight. If you are using a wet glue or paste, change waste sheets as necessary to absorb moisture.

Liquor Shower Variation

Of course it doesn't have to be a cookbook—you could make a book of cocktails instead.

I heard about coed liquor showers when Dikko and I got married. Everyone brings two bottles of liquor: one for the party, one for the couple, so that they will have a well-stocked liquor cabinet. Dikko's friends threw one for us. It was a surprise, and I was more than surprised—I was shocked. My heart didn't stop racing for an hour (I think surprise parties for the elderly or a person with a heart condition—or even pregnant women—could be seriously dangerous).

In this era of mixology, that idea could go further, with cocktail shakers and other cool tools. There was a lot of funky cocktail stuff midcentury—so an eBay or Etsy or vintage-shop approach can be a fun way to do this. This is another opportunity to think about your style. Is it elegant ornate, sleek designer modern, funky vintage?

You can make a **flag book** (page 70), but here are two other options: a **stab stitch**, binding single pieces of paper, and a **pamphlet**, or **chap book**, with a sheaf of paper that you fold and stitch on the fold.

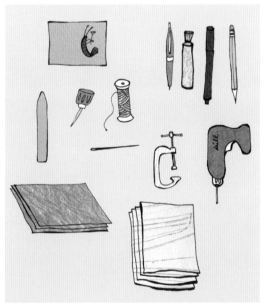

Materials

Cocktail recipe *from each of your shower guests*

Thin paper *for the interior that feeds easily through your photocopier or computer printer*

Black pens, soft pencils, or markers, *if people are handwriting*

Thicker, foldable paper *for the covers*

Drill *and* clamps *(for stab-stitch version)*

Decorative paper *for end sheets (optional, but nice)*

Bone folder

Needle, linen thread,

awl *(for pamphlet version)*

Diagram of Variations on Variations

(on a gift to give the bethrothed)

Shower Book

Cookbook   Cocktails

Flag   Stab   Pamphlet

Computer   Photocopy   One of a Kind

Via computer:

Figure out who will function as editor/designer/organizer. A few people may want to collaborate. My friend Chris says the secret of good collaboration is to work with people who have different strengths. Is anyone a graphic designer? Anyone have access to a color printer?

1 **Have everyone e-mail his or her favorite cocktail recipe in advance. This could be in a word-processing program that everyone has, or just pasted into an e-mail.**

2 **Choose a size for the book. Fold a piece of standard-size photocopy paper to see what looks good. You could fold vertically or horizontally or in quarters. You could also cut it smaller on any side.**

Some people prefer to avoid any size that is obviously based on copier paper—you could go square, for example, if you want to trim at the end, though that could be difficult. Do you really want to trim each book by hand? You could see if your local copy shop can do this for you. That standard size begins to look more attractive . . .

3 **Plan for wide margins. Photocopiers stretch and shrink, so don't have any of your words or pictures close to the edges. Bleed is the word used in the industry for printing that comes close to the edge of the page—bleed requires custom trimming, so it always costs extra. If you want anything close to the edge, you will need to allow space on the page and extra time for trimming.**

NOTE: If you want people to handwrite their pages, give them a few pieces of paper to work with, in case they make a mistake. You could send this with instructions as part of the invitation.

If you are just making just one stab-stitch book for the couple—fold the same margin on each piece of paper and have each person write his or her drink recipe on it. We have used pads of art paper for books like this, separating the pages and distributing a page or two to each participant.

If you will print on a photocopier, have them write in black on white paper. When you photocopy, use any color papers you like. If you are using a color photocopier, or scanning pages in with a color computer printer, anything goes (color-wise).

Inkjet printers can take a variety of paper. A young designer just showed me her portfolio of books she'd made feeding heavily textured handmade paper through her inkjet printer. The feel was lovely—experiment with whatever papers appeal to you.

Remember—get all your drink recipes several weeks in advance so you have time to organize. Things go wrong—it's normal. Expect it. Give yourself plenty of leeway (in time and materials).

For a stab-stitch book—
SINGLE SHEETS ARE PILED UP AND SEWN AT THE SPINE

1   **Design your recipe pages with a big margin on the left. It's best if your paper is wider than it is long.**

If you are photocopying multiple copies, plan to work on standard photocopy paper—but you could set up more than one book page per sheet.

NOTE: You can reuse one-sided paper for this book, printing on the backs of already-printed paper and then folding the paper and sewing shut at the spine as shown.

2   **Pile up your sheets, add covers, clamp, and drill a few holes a little bit in from the spine, according to that margin you had planned. Stitch as shown, taking your thread around and through the spine. Practice this first to be sure it works. Then alter as necessary and continue.**

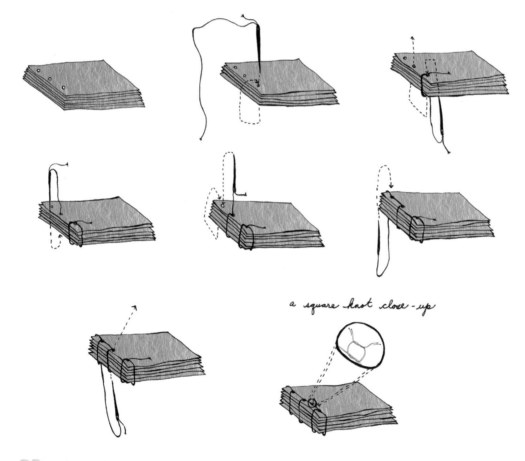

a square knot close-up

OR staple. You'd need access to a heavy-duty stapler that can go through all those sheets of paper.

OR use paper bolts from stationery stores—paper bolts have two pieces that screw together. Well-equipped copy shops can help with this.

OR punch holes and tie with ribbons.

OR use binding rings, if you'd like a loose-leaf feel.

For a pamphlet, or chap book—

A SIMPLE BOOK MADE FROM ONE SIGNATURE, A SINGLE, FOLDED SECTION OF PAPER

PAMPHLET STITCH

1 For a pamphlet, or chap book—a simple book made from one signature, a single, folded section of paper, you need to plan carefully so your pages back up correctly. First make a dummy book, or a mock-up. This is a process that publishers and book designers use for planning. How many pages do you want? Remember one folded sheet of paper equals four pages.

How many pages will fit on your "press"? For photocopy, your standard paper sizes are your base. How many pages will fit on the size you choose—either letter size or legal size, or, depending on your machine, maybe larger? Cut and fold cheap paper (even reuse paper), the number of pages you think you will need for your book. "Bind" the pages with a rubber band. Number your pages and scribble what will go on each one. If the book is going to contain favorite drink recipes from a group of friends, you could write their names on the dummy to indicate where their cocktails will go. Add or decrease pages according to your needs. Do you want to add illustrations, clip art, collages, or photos? Don't forget about a title page—and if there are extra pages in the back, that can be for notes and writing in other recipes later.

2 When you have figured out your dummy book, take it apart, and if the pages are cut down from the full-size sheet, lightly tape them back together. Use that as a guide to lay out your master pages. If someone is doing this on a computer, this will be the guide for their design. Otherwise, very carefully paste up the originals into the format. Then try photocopying one copy to be sure it works—cut it and fold it and rubber-band and double-check. If it's good, print as many as you need onto your good paper (sometimes the cheap paper prints better than nice paper, so check one before you do them all).

3 Trim as needed, fold, add decorative end sheets, and a cover, made of heavier but foldable paper. You can print or photocopy onto the cover. Or make a label, photocopy it, and stick it on.

4 Then bind. I prefer to stitch by hand with needle and linen thread. To do this, punch three holes with an awl—one in the middle and one a bit in from the top and the other a bit in from the bottom. Stitch in a B shape—out through the middle, leaving a long tail, in through the top or bottom, skip the middle, out through the top or bottom, and back in the middle, on the other side of that long stitch. Adjust the tension—pulling with care so your thread doesn't rip through your paper. Tie AROUND the long stitch with a square knot (left over right, right over left) so the knot won't work its way out.

Stitching these books can be part of the shower entertainment. Or have a smaller binding party ahead of time. You can make this into a commemorative party favor for everyone who attends the liquor shower.

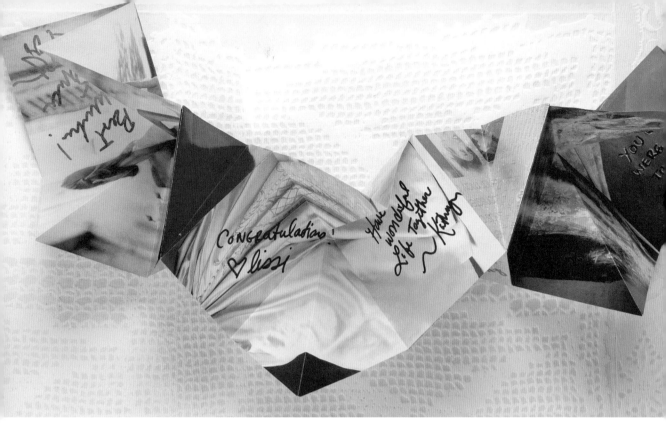

Garland Guest Book

A guest book or a decorative garland? It's both! This book is also called a snake book—Anna Wolf, who lives and works in the San Francisco Bay area and is active in the book-arts community there, is credited with its invention—or discovery—some of these forms just sort of happen.

Make these as long as you like—they're perfect for something open-ended where people might forget to participate! We made ours reusing pages from some bridal magazines—but use whatever papers appeal to you—they just need to be thin enough to fold. Use colors that make sense with your wedding. Paper is a great way to try color ideas—a much smaller investment than bridesmaid's gowns (or even fancy flowers from a florist).

You could have two colors of paper for people to write on—one for the bride and one for groom—and then alternate them in the long garland. Or use many colors of paper—or cut from bridal magazines (as we did), which you could intersperse with plain paper. You can even make this project from the wrapping paper if the bride is a careful unwrapper—me, I always rip open presents to see what's inside.

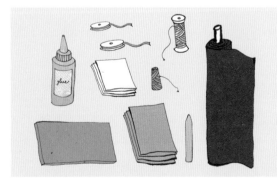

We reused bridal magazines for this origami garland.

Materials

SQUARES OF FOLDABLE PAPER

BONE FOLDER

ADHESIVE

HEAVY-WEIGHT PAPER OR BOARD FOR COVER

PAPER or BOOK CLOTH *to cover board (optional, instructions on page 19)*

RIBBONS or STRINGS

1. Mail squares of paper with the shower invitations—or hand the squares out at the party for people to write on. You can choose a theme—like advice for a happy marriage or wishes or drawings of the bride and groom—or just have guests sign their names. Even if you mail the squares, have extras at the party just in case—weddings (and life?) are all about having extras just in case!

2. Fold the paper diagonally so that the message shows—open and fold horizontally and vertically, hiding the message. Pop so that the point sticks up and the paper folds into a neat little tucked-in diagonal square. The messages should be on the inside of the folded pieces. Note: If you would like to use collage, fold the squares and glue collage pieces before you send them to guests so that they avoid the folds.

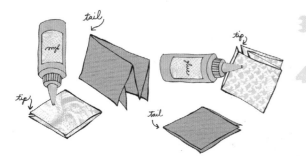

3. Glue the squares together tip to tail, closed point to open point, as shown.

4. For your covers, cut heavy paper or boards the size of the folded pieces (one-quarter the size of your original squares). Cover the boards if you like (instructions on page 19).

5. At both ends of the garland, glue ribbons or strings to stick out on both ends between the pages and the covers. Glue your covers over the ribbons—burnish well and let dry under weight. (This drying step is a good reason to make the garland BEFORE the party—you could have a pre-party book-making party!).

6. Open and extend the garland to its full length and find a good place to hang it for party décor—if you do not burnish well enough or give it time to dry under weight, it might come apart (guess how I know this!)—but it is easy to repair.

Table Runners

Once when I was teaching a workshop, we made these as a variation of the Garland Guest Book (page 78)—they are also based on origami forms, but inside out. I told my students I thought they'd be great for nuts and candy—so here they are!

Cutting magazine paper (from bridal magazines!) for this project can look interesting and is a great way to reuse paper. Any stiff foldable paper will work.

Materials

SQUARES OF PAPER, *approximately 6" (15 cm) but it can vary*

BONE FOLDER

ADHESIVE

1 **Take a square of paper and fold it horizontally. Turn the paper over and fold it diagonally in both directions, so that the folds form an X. Push the sides in so that a triangle with symmetrical pleats forms, as shown. Fold eight or more of these.**

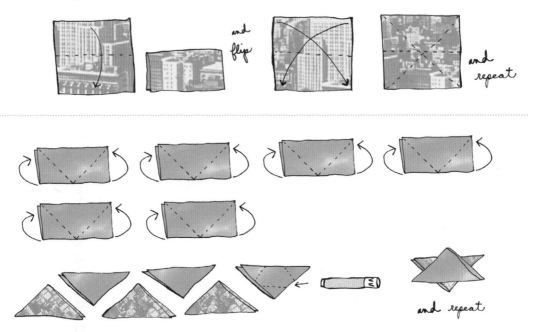

2 **Glue your folded triangles together right side up/upside down so that the two triangles form a six-pointed star. Burnish and dry under weight and then gently pull apart to make a runner that can hold dry snacks—pistachio nuts, dried fruit, small pretzels, candies, bridge mix, Jordan almonds . . .**

NOTE: Book weights can be any heavy clean flat thing to weight down your paper so that it will hold its folds. You can fill flat-bottomed tins with pennies, wrap bricks or cinderblocks in cloth or paper like presents, use old stovetop flat irons, put a brick in an old sock. I have geode bookends that make excellent book weights—a wedding gift from my sister-in-law, Sheri.

{ **We re-used magazine paper for this table runner. Polly picked up the pistachios.**

Chapter 4
Ceremony

*I*t is the day you've been preparing for,
when everyone comes together.

Everything that can go wrong will go wrong—and it will all bring you luck.

We'd planned for an outdoor wedding. So, of course, it rained for the first time in months. A violent thunderstorm—torrents. We had to delay the ceremony so that people could drive in. We had planned to be married on a little stone bridge. Luckily, there was a big, old-fashioned porch instead.

I worked in theater then. I was used to tech rehearsals, to solving all the problems, to having control of the situation. That doesn't happen with weddings. But the emotion of the event can carry it pretty far. At our wedding several men fell in love with the same woman. They were calling me for weeks afterwards. She chose one of them and they've been together ever since—so our anniversary is their love-at-first-sight anniversary.

It will be wonderful, whatever happens, but it shouldn't be the happiest day of your life. You don't want the rest of your life to go downhill from there. You want to live happily ever after!

{ **Susan Springer Anderson used** *New York Times* **magazines for the paper bride's dress.**

Paper Flowers

These remind me of the Flowers for Mother we made from Kleenex in elementary school for Mother's Day. Ashley Soliman made these elegant 1920s-inspired versions. You can make them as large or as small as you like. Experiment and keep in mind the architectural aspects of paper—like a doll house versus a playhouse versus a real house, the bigger the house, the thicker the walls—a tiny flower needs thinner paper than a huge one does.

I've broken the flowers down into two basics design—the Concertina Flower and the Petticoat Flower. And I'm also giving you several headdress projects you can try making with these flower designs—and I do recommend trying them out quickly to see what you like making. But don't stop with these ideas—try out your own variations—make centerpieces with these flowers, make boutonnieres for the groomsmen—make favors, make long ropes of them and hang them from the rafters. Have fun.

Materials

THIN PAPERS—*tissue, waxed paper, recycled bridal magazines, one-sided printer paper (flowers with text/patterns look really interesting)*

ADHESIVE—*glue, wheat paste (recipe on page 128), glue stick, or double-stick tape*

THREAD *and/or* PIPE CLEANERS *and/or* FLORIST'S WIRE *(depends on what you will make with your flowers)*

PAPER CLIPS

WASTE SHEETS

RIBBONS, HEADBANDS, ETC.

{ Ashley Soliman reused magazine pages and wrapping paper for these paper flowers.

Concertina Flower

1 Cut your paper: The basic fan flower starts with a strip of paper in a 1:3 ratio—so 3 5/8" (or so) x 11" (9 x 28 cm). Try this out with your recycling scraps. You could also do 3" x 9" (7.5 x 23 cm) or 4" x 12" (10 x 30.5 cm) or 10" x 30" (25.5 x 76 cm), depending on the scale you would like for your flowers. Even 1" x 3" (2.5 x 7.5 cm) is possible—but remember that the smaller your piece, the thinner the paper should be (tissue paper would be good for tiny ones), and the larger your flower, the thicker the paper—though some paper just won't fold.

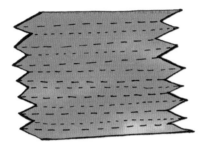

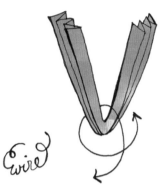

2 Accordion-fold your paper into a narrow concertina (a small accordion fold) turning it every time so that you don't fold more than one layer at a time. You can play with other ratios and other amounts of accordion folds and see how you like the results. Keep in mind paper grain (more on page 27). When you fold, TAKE THE PATH OF LEAST RESISTANCE!

3 Fold your concertina in half and tie or stitch it in the center with wire or thread.

4 Glue (or double-stick-tape) the concertina ends together around your thread to keep the flower open—use a paper clip to hold it while the glue sets. Note: If your paper is very thin, like tissue, use a waste sheet between that first accordion fold and the next fold so that your glue doesn't bleed through.

VARIATION

Snip the tips of the folded accordion before you open your flower (as shown) OR snip into the accordion for a snowflake effect.

Petticoat Flower

1 Stack ten or more pieces of tissue paper, cut into rough circles of any size.

2 Poke holes through the center and anchor the circles with wire, pipe cleaner, or thread to be sewn button style.

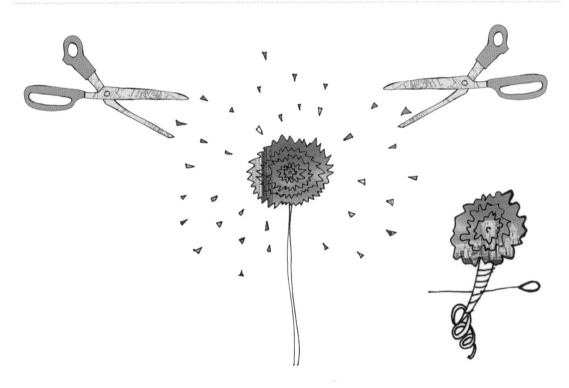

3 Crumple one layer at a time and then fluff them up. OR you can chop at the edges and fluff for a more carnation-like flower.

4 Use florist's wire to make this into an elegant boutonniere.

Headdresses

Ashley made these lovely headdresses with her flowers—great for flower girls and bridesmaids, as well as the bride. You could have a paper-flower-making tea or shower. And/or wear them at a shower if something less papery appeals to you for the actual wedding.

The Fascinator

Flower Ribbon

Flower Crown

The Fascinator

1 Make a Concertina Flower from an approximately 5" x 15" (12.5 x 38 cm) strip of paper.

2 Make a Petticoat Flower from approximately 2" (5 cm) circles.

3 Sew the Petticoat Flower through the spaces of the Concertina Flower onto about 1 yard (91 cm) of ¹⁄₄" (6 mm) ribbon.

Tie it on like a tiny tam—or fascinator (those 1920s frothy little hats), as shown in the photo.

Flower Ribbon

Sew six or more small Petticoat Flowers, centered on a ribbon about 1 ½ to 2 yards long and 1" wide (137–183 cm long and 2.5 cm wide). Use as a headdress or a belt.

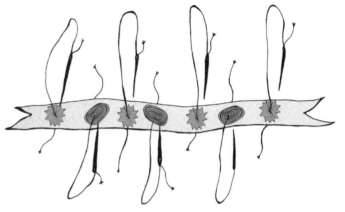

Flower Crown

1. Make a Concertina Flower from a wider proportion piece of paper. Try 7" x 11" (18 x 28 cm) if you are using standard office paper as your base—or play with this idea, trying out the form before you commit to a design and paper choice.

2. Accordion-fold or pleat into sixteen sections (in half and in half again and again, reversing the folds as you go—fold only one layer of paper at a time).

3. Fold your pleated concertina in half and glue the top together, forming a semicircle.

4. Unfold one fold at the bottom, wrap around a 2" (5 cm) ribbon, and adhere. This makes a platform.

5. You can add a second flower—it should have the same number of folds as the first—but this one can be more cut out, like paper lace (you could even try using a paper lace doilies).

6. For a front decorative piece, fold a strip of paper to attach to the ribbon platform. Open, accor-dion-old, and cut away—snowflake style—cutting down to the platform hinge piece, so that it can curve around the head with the ribbon.

7. Glue or stitch onto the platform/ribbon.

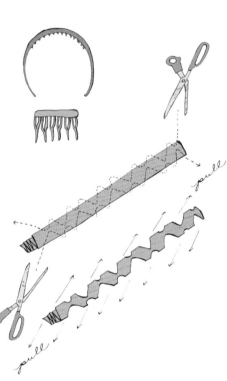

pleated tissue paper

Paper Veil

1 Pleat a full-size sheet of tissue paper, and cut out simple shapes—like triangles—in from both sides, alternating.

2 Open carefully—the paper lace will stretch. Attach one end to a headband or comb. You can attach a semicircle Concertina Flower or other paper flowers for further embellishment.

You could use this paper lace to wrap a bouquet (of real or paper flowers).

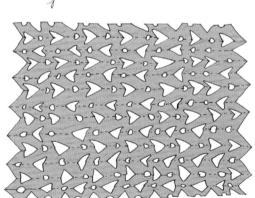

PAPER DRESS

As I was thinking about *The Paper Bride*, I really wanted to include a bride's dress made from bridal magazines and society pages. Paper dresses were quite the thing when I was a kid, and I ordered a Yellow Pages dress for 99¢ from the back of a magazine. I put it on when it arrived and went to the shopping center (in those pre-mall days) with my dad. It tore under the sleeve within half an hour. This was crazy because, of course, a paper dress would tear—but then why did they sell them? Too bad I didn't just keep it in its original package—I'll bet a mint-condition paper dress would sell for a pretty penny on eBay.

My editors do not think anyone would actually want to wear a paper dress to their wedding. After my experience with my Yellow Pages dress, I can understand why you might not.

Plus this one was very time-consuming to make. I was fortunate to find Susan Springer Anderson, an artist who specializes in making paper dresses as sculptures and installation pieces. I visited her studio, just to look at her work, to see how I would make one. Then I asked if she would want to make one for the book and she said yes—I felt as if I'd won the lottery! I've been so lucky to have the participation of many artists who made things or let me borrow their things to photograph for my books—but someone I didn't know who was willing to spend months working out the details of making a paper bridal gown?—well, I'm just very grateful.

Susan built *The Paper Bride*'s dress on a dress form. At first, she tried making this dress from the *New York Times* Style sections, but found that the newsprint discolored so quickly that the paper was darker every time she came back to her studio. So she switched to the coated *New York Times Magazine*, which has more longevity. The large size of the magazine also worked better because she didn't have to piece together smaller pages. And the crossword puzzles are such a nice touch . . . I love the way the paper catches the light with its silk-like sheen.

If you do decide to wear a paper dress, wear a very nice slip under it. A reused-paper dress would certainly lessen the carbon footprint of your wedding. (Is there such a thing as a negative carbon footprint?)

Susan Springer Anderson "constructed and attached everything using a glue stick, mod podge, or a hot glue gun."

"I couldn't sew in a zipper so the dress closes with Velcro.

First I experimented with different designs for the dress. I tried to work with the character traits of the paper. There are certain forms it just refused to take. So once I had kind of gotten a handle on how the paper naturally wanted to fold, I was able to narrow down the design.

I began with the skirt. I laid out large sections of the newspaper and glued pieces end to end, making long strips. Then I overlapped them side to side to create a semicircle. That made the underskirt. Then I folded the New York Times magazine pages into individual ruffles and then glued them edge to edge to create one long ruffle. I made several rows of these. Then I attached them to the underskirt."

Wedding Programs

Your wedding program can include some or all of the following: names, date, place, order of ceremony, readings, music, officiant, wedding party, acknowledgments, and thank-yous . . .

Programs can take many forms—from a single one-sided sheet with beautiful typography to something more elaborate like the ones in this photo that Jennifer King made—an accordion, a pamphlet (instructions page 109), and the fan project that follows.

For any program, you need to start the same way with a few basics. First, you write the words and decide how you'd like to typeset them. You will lay this out in black on white paper if you are photocopying. You could handwrite (see the Handwriting Guide on page 130). Or typeset on a computer or even a typewriter if you can find one.

You could use a graphic-design computer program—but it's not necessary. Some of Jennifer's samples in the photo were made before computer graphics were common. She cut and pasted the type to fit the format and photocopied it onto interesting paper.

For the illustrations or little ornaments, you could either use computer dingbats or clip art or photocopy pictures from antique books. You are sort of making a collage from black on white sources. When you photocopy, your designs look like a single piece. You may have to adjust your photocopier's contrast and possibly touch up the cut edges of your original—or the cut marks on a photocopy—and then recopy it. Use Pro White or some other correction fluid. When I used Pro White, I was advised to let it dry and then use it like watercolor with a brush dipped in water.

If you are working in a large copy shop, they may have a work area with tools and materials for you to use.

If you need to use a copy shop, ask around to find a good one. When I made the photocopy thank-you notes and holiday cards after my wedding (photo on page 65) I got to know the people in my copy shop. My favorite clerk was an opera singer—he had an amazingly beautiful voice—the copy shop was his day job. He got interested in my projects and was a great help. Some of the huge chain stores pay everyone in the nation the same rate—so you get much better service if you live in a part of the country where people can survive on minimum wage.

{ **Jennifer King used photocopy and computer printer to make these programs.**

Program Fan

Materials

INTERESTING CARD STOCK IN STANDARD PRINT SIZE—*check to make sure it will go through your photocopy machine or computer*

RIBBON

HOLE PUNCH

TEMPLATE *(page 138)—or design your own shape*

1 Make a dummy/sketch/mock-up and try out the shape—figure that two "leaves" of the fan will fit on a piece of standard-size copier/printer paper.

2 Write you information and design it. Type it on a computer or even a typewriter if you can find one. Or handwrite it (handwriting guide page 130). Or have someone do it for you—ask for handwriting services as a wedding gift. Some teenage girls have wonderful handwriting—as do elderly aunts—especially if they went to parochial school!

3 Print and cut.

4 Punch holes—you can grommet if you like, but I like it better without.

5 Tie with ribbon—if your ribbon is a bit wider than your hole, it will hold the fan together. Again, try this out with some variations to see what you like best before you buy all your ribbon and go into production. You can make the ribbon long enough so that the fan can hang on your wrist.

This fan could, alternatively, work as a save-the-date—and would also make an excellent menu.

Chapter 5
Reception

From a bottle of champagne popped and poured at a picnic,

or cupcakes on the Brooklyn Bridge, to a buffet with a deejay or a formal sit-down dinner and a dance band

—your reception could be almost anything—as long as it's festive.

Whatever your style, elaborateness (and budget!), you will probably want a guest book—or something for that purpose. Assuming you'll have photos—formal, professional, or snaps from people's phones—you may need a photo album.

If you are having tables, do you want to seat your guests? I encourage table number alternatives so that no one feels left out sitting at table 17. Try something more interesting. Instead of table numbers, you could have a different theme—Greek islands, New York City landmarks, flowers, animals, colors, whatever. Though even with those there is an equivalent to number 17—after the roses and violets and daisies and tulips, you could run out of popular flowers and be left with the weeds. But I love dandelions—wish I knew a way to keep them from wilting so fast.

{ **Georgia Luna hand-lettered the place cards; Lissi laser printed the coaster onto cardstock.**

⌐ **Georgia Luna made the place cards in the photo on this page—she got creative with odd sizes of paper. See what looks nice with the other elements on your table and have fun!**

Place Cards

Place cards or table cards can be done many ways. When we are making wedding invitations for people, I look at how the paper cuts down and fits on the press and design a place card for whatever size we have left over. Sometimes we print on a little picture—or a typographic element—initials, date, even a beautiful ampersand—as a visual element on the place cards. OR the paper color and texture and writing style can be enough.

If you want them to stand, you can fold them several ways. Tent folds are pretty common—and soooo easy—just take a rectangle of paper and fold it in half. To decide the size or shape, check your list for the longest name and design around that. Sample templates are on page 137.

People sometimes write the names of the guests on little envelopes and stuff them with cards that have the table number (or flower or breed of dog, if you are getting creative in your table naming). There are nice, small envelopes commercially available—some come with cards to fit. But you can make your own (page 34)—OR you can line commercial envelopes (page 36). These envelopes will not go through the mail, so make an unglued version if you like.

Another folding option for standing place cards is to take long strips of paper and fold in one or both edges. Again, check the longest name on your list—Laura Carmelita Bellmont takes up more space than Sue Pitt. Cut and fold your paper big enough for the longest name.

You can handwrite these (see handwriting guide page 130)—or hire a professional calligrapher or the friend or family member you've designated as your official calligrapher. Test the pens on the paper you intend to use to be sure the ink doesn't bleed in some odd way.

Liz Zanis made these irreverent place cards on her computer.

Another approach is to take your list and set it up in the computer in a typeface that is the same or compatible with your invitation, or some other piece you've used. To do that, base your size on a standard printer paper size—you have the most options with 8.5" x 11" (21.5 x 28 cm)—so fold a piece down and see what makes the most sense and then try some configurations with your list. I don't like to say TRIAL & ERROR—but you do need to go through some proofing and trimming down to see what will work best for this.

Napkin Rings

Georgia Luna also made these napkin rings. I've always liked the idea of napkin rings that also function as place cards—but you can also add an image—rubber stamp can work for this—or just cut a nice shape from beautiful paper. I've given you a template for this napkin ring that slits together (see page 136). You probably will do best with a cover-weight paper for these—but experiment with anything you think is pretty—even a translucent vellum might look nice. Try your own variations of this idea, changing the shape to go with your décor—another (small and easy) opportunity to make your wedding your own.

Paper Lanterns

These can be as elegant or as funky as you like. They can be any size—tiny to go over fairy lights or strikingly large. Or try a combination of many sizes, some for your tables, others for hanging from strings or ribbons from above. Make a quick one from that pile of scrap paper first to try it out. You could make these long before the reception and then keep them flat and finish assembling when you decorate later—but try assembling a few so that you know what you are doing.

Materials

FOLDABLE PAPER, RECTANGLES (*though you can try any shape to see how you like it*)

SCISSORS

STAPLER, TAPE, or GLUE—or a HOLE PUNCH *if you'd like to weave the lanterns with ribbons or strips of paper*

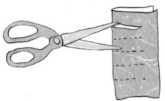

1 Fold the paper in half. Cut even, parallel lines in from the fold toward the opposite edge, leaving a margin of about a quarter of the paper.

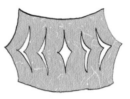

2 Open the cut paper and curve it together, stapling top and bottom.

3 Add a strip at the top, stapled on both sides, as a hanger.

4 Now that you've tried it and "get" it—think about how you want to use the lantern—should it be tiny, huge, various sizes?

You can make them from elegant paper or simple paper, or reuse paper—from bridal magazines or society pages. The larger the lanterns are, the heavier the paper needs to be; the smaller, the more delicate. You can make them very simple or vary the cuts and try some patterns.

Instead of stapling, you can use double-stick tape or glue that won't show—or punch holes and thread a strip of paper through for a woven pattern—or try a combination—thread the paper OVER staples, so your lanterns will stay together while you decorate.

Remember that paper can burn (I don't want to hear on the news about your wedding going up in flames!), so don't use these with candles—but you could put them around electric candles. The Museum of Modern Art had some beautiful electric candles.

VARIATION: You can paint your paper before you cut. Test your paper to see how it responds to paint—some papers buckle when wet—you may even want to use watercolor paper. Even brushing lightly with a wide brush dipped in a little gold acrylic can give a nice effect. Or try paste paper for these (see page 128).

{ **Painter Stephanie Brody-Lederman embellished these magazine-paper lanterns with paint, ribbons, and artificial birds, leaves and flowers.**

Cake Toppers

Our intern, Ashley, who made the paper flowers on page 84, played with my paper cake topper idea and tried a few things, but nothing quite worked. Polly took over the project at the last minute and did a slight variation of Ashley's design and that did the trick. (The template for this is on page 139.)

There are many interesting variations for cake toppers. One bride we knew painted tiny spectacles on a ceramic cake topper since she and the groom both wore glasses. When I was first engaged, a woman who ran a little store in Chicago gave me a vintage porcelain bride and groom—they were sweet and beautiful, and I still keep them on a shelf. But we forgot them when we went to Pennsylvania for the wedding. None of our friends had keys to our apartment (make a note—be sure to leave keys with someone in case you forget something!). So instead they improvised—one friend brought clear blue space aliens. And my flower girl provided tiny painted wooden toy people—lots of things can work—but if you are truly the paper bride— get some black-and-white card stock or thick, but foldable art papers and cut out the pattern for Ashley and Polly's design.

Cake Boxes

Many years ago, I attended my friends Marv and Anne Marie's wedding. Anne Marie's mother was English and had made a traditional wedding fruitcake. That was before fruitcake was so maligned by standup comedians, and I loved it. At the end of the reception, unmarried women each got a tiny box with a small square of cake. We were told to sleep with it under our pillow that night so that we would dream of the man we would marry. I was taking an all-night train to Chicago, and I tried to sleep on it—but don't remember a dream. In the end I ate it for a snack. When Dikko and I got married a few years later, I asked Mrs. Fetterman for the recipe, and she also lent her tiered cake pans. Luckily, my friend Becky was dating a former football player who helped stir the batter—it took muscle!

I loved the box idea, so wanted to include some. The easiest option is to buy bakery boxes and decorate them. Polly did this one with rubber stamps. If you are more ambitious, you could make your own boxes, cutting and assembling them with the template on page 134. Find a beautiful color and texture paper that goes with your other decor. Leave the boxes plain, or stamp them, or even embellish with printed labels, stickers, collage. And, of course, you can tie the boxes with ribbon—a table of bow-topped boxes could be another lovely element.

Coasters

Typical coaster board is so thick that it's very hard to cut. And it barely bends around the cylinder of our press—let alone a computer printer. You could stencil it or print it with photocopy transfer. But I worried that it is really something better to have professionally printed and die cut. Then Stephanie Brody-Lederman gave me a coaster she'd picked up in Paris. It has an interesting sort of Art Nouveau shape—Lissi says it looks like it was drawn with a French curve (which I guess they must use in Paris!) It was printed on regular paper—something more like card stock than coaster board. A perfect solution!

Lissi made her own version of it, scanning her engagement necklace and trying some things with initials. She set up as many as she could fit on a page, laser-printed (inkjet might bleed with dampness) and hand-cut them. She recommends testing your paper (I always recommend testing everything)—before you make them all.

That little yellow box (template on page 135) can hold a single chocolate as a wedding favor.

Thaumotrope

Thaumotropes (or spinners) can be good favors or even thank-you note inserts. *Magic Books & Paper Toys* features these—but here is a method to edition them—print a bunch on your computer or photocopier, on a paper that you will fold to make it thicker two-sided, without having to make it register. They could also be great fun as save-the-dates.

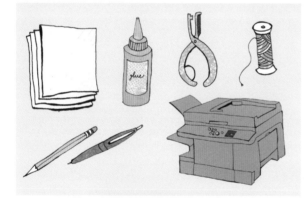

Materials

HEAVY, FOLDABLE CARD STOCK—8.5" x 11" (21.5 x 28 cm)—*some to design with and then more for printing*

HOLE PUNCHER OR GLUE

THREAD OR STRING

PENCIL/PEN

PHOTOCOPY MACHINE

GLUE

1 Take a piece of foldable card stock that is double the desired length of your thaumotrope. Fold it in half.

2 Find the center of the paper and punch holes (or if you'd rather attach your string with glue, then pencil in a mark to indicate the center). Check that your thaumotrope works when you twirl it—just rub it between your thumb and forefinger—you don't need to twist the string.

⌐ Liz Zanis printed her Just Married subway thaumotrope via computer.

3 Lightly pencil a design on each side—right side up/upside down. The classic thaumotrope has a bird on one side and an upside-down cage on the other. When you twirl it, the afterimage puts the bird inside the cage. For a wedding thaumotrope, initials can join with an ampersand—split as you like—& on one side, initials on the other? Or one initial on each side. Or take a picture of the two of you, cut it in half, and put one person on each side.

Experiment with some images. Ball and chain—if you are into tasteless wedding humor.

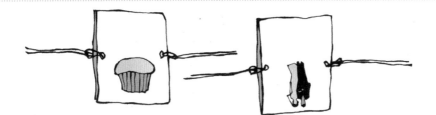

4 When you are happy with your sketch, when the animation/afterimage really works—go over the lines with pen and ink or very dark marker.

You will need to glue the two sides together, but first, you will need to reproduce your original.

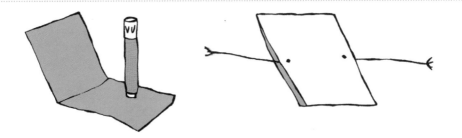

5 To do this, unfold your original and print it on foldable paper. Cut the photocopies to size, fold, and then glue front to back—the string can be glued to the inside, or put through punched holes.

When I made these with my class, a student said, "These are delightful!" I realized that they were the Game Boy or iPhones of their era. (Victorian times are as far back as I've traced them.) People haven't changed—we've always enjoyed handheld amusement devices—only the technology changed.

And, like learning to use your new phone, you need to learn to twirl these. They are rare now, so people don't always know how. If you send them through the mail, you may need to include instructions. But they may be making a comeback. I got a New Year's card with one just the other day.

Pamphlet Guest Book

A student of mine gave me a notebook from India that had a wonderful solution to lined pages. The pages were folded and then flattened out so that the creases made lines—it's a technique I've used many times for quick books. One year, we scored a datebook on our press to make that look for a whole edition. The book needs no words, but if you like, before you start the whole process, you could write or typeset some text and photocopy or print it out on all your sheets before you begin.

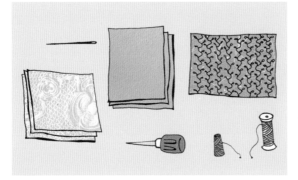

Materials

Lightweight paper

Cover-weight paper

End sheets

Awl

Needle

Linen thread

1 Decide on what size book you'd like. You could use 8 1/2" x 11" (21.5 x 28 cm) paper for a 5 1/2" x 8 1/2" book or 4 1/4" x 11" [11 x 28 cm] for a tall, narrow book, or anything you like. Just remember that your page will be half the size of your paper when you fold it for the binding. Your cover should be a little larger than your page, since when you fold the sheets, the thickness of the paper adds up. So if you are using 8 1/2" x 11" (21.5 x 28 cm) paper— use 8 1/2" x 14" (21.5 x 35.5 cm) cover stock to fold around the insides. You can either trim the ends to fit, or fold them in for an elegant flap.

Endpapers, like covers, need to be a little wider than the text sheets for the same reason. End sheets are optional in a pamphlet book, but they are a nice touch—they are one of my favorite things about books. You can buy decorative paper or make your own (see the recipe for paste papers on page 128).

Decide how many sheets you want for your guest book. This binding makes sense for a smallish wedding. Do you want to use a whole page per person, half a page, a quarter? Or have a bunch of people sign on the same page?

Each sheet of paper becomes four sheets when you fold it in half to bind—so if you have fifty wedding guests—and you want to have two people sign per page, you'll divide 25 pages by 4—but since 25 doesn't divide evenly by 4—and 28 does—you'll need seven pieces of thin paper (7 x 4 = 28)—this will give you some extra for a title page, or whatever you like.

{ I used the Ethiopian Coptic stitch (page 116) for the top left book. The top right was made for Dikko and me by our Center for Book Arts friends, and I made the bottom one accordion-scoring handmade paper as shown on page 110.

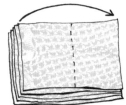

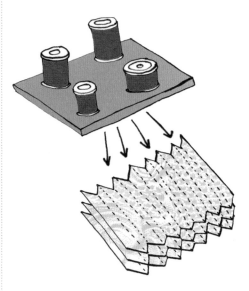

2 Start by making your signature. Pile up your sheets, straighten them, and fold them in half, careful to line them up so they form a point at the fore-edge.

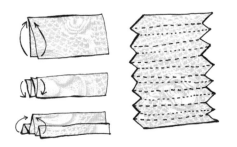

3 To make the lines, accordion-fold your paper horizontally, folding in half and halving the folds again and again until you like the thickness of the lines. Test this out with a recycled piece of paper before you use your good paper. Alternatively, fold a pleat that you like and accordion-fold the whole sheet to match. Turn the paper over as you fold. With lightweight paper, you should be able to fold several sheets at a time. These folds will create the lines for people to sign on—they don't need to be super-precise.

Repeat until you have folded all the sheets.

You may also want to have some vertical lines—to separate name, address, etc.—so choose those dimensions and fold something you like.

4 Again try out your folds on scrap paper first.

After you've done all your folding, flatten the paper and put it under weight overnight or for a few hours so that it gets used to being flat again. You could even iron it if you like (try one sheet first to test that idea). I pretty much never iron—though sometimes I iron things for books—if I can FIND my iron—

5 Then fold the paper into your signature again. Lay your end sheets and cover around your signature.

6 Make three holes with an awl, one in the middle, one pretty close to the top, and one pretty close to the bottom. You can take a strip of paper the height of the book and fold it in half to find the center and then fold in about an inch (2.5 cm) from your folded ends, so that your holes are symmetrical—OR (as I usually do with things like this) eyeball it.

8 Stitch from the inside out at the middle hole, reserving thread to tie later, come back in the top or bottom, skip the middle, go out the other end, and go back in the middle, making a B stitch (NOT a figure 8!). Careful—don't split your thread when you come back in the middle. Put the thread ends around the long center thread so that one is on each side and tie a square knot—left over right and right over left. Trim and voilà! You could leave a very long thread and tie a pen to it if you like.

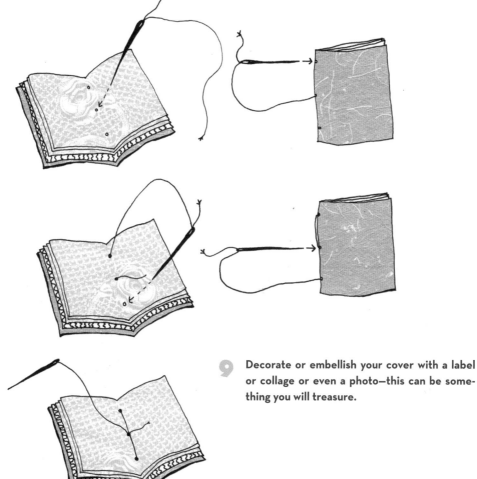

9 Decorate or embellish your cover with a label or collage or even a photo—this can be something you will treasure.

Some people ask their guests to draw a picture of them. Or you could come up with a question for them to answer—or just hope for some creative input.

Some people like to have more control than a guest book offers. One option is to find a pretty box and give people pieces of paper to write on and put them into the box (more about this on page 112). Or cut card stock for people to sign and incorporate the pieces into your photo album later on. Or make a flag book (page 70) from the pieces of paper that you've had people sign.

Put someone in charge of the guest book (this can be a good job for a responsible child) to be sure everyone signs.

Depending on the style of your wedding—you may want to have colored markers to encourage creativity—or you could have pens printed with your names and the wedding date that will be favors as well as being useful for this project.

Your guest book can become a conversation piece; it can be in an area where people can go for a little quiet time between dances.

GUEST BOOK BOX OF CARDS

Some people skip the guest book and have a box of precut cards for people to sign—and write personal notes to you on. Find a box that you like and cut the cards to match. You can choose one color of paper—like a nice warm white—or use a variety of colors that look beautiful as part of your wedding, picking up colors that you use in the flowers or attendants' dresses.

Pens also can be very simple, black or dark blue—or can be a variety of colors to encourage creative additions. A writing or drawing area can be a nice place of respite at a reception—just be sure someone is watching over it, so it doesn't get out of control. If children will be there, make an area just for them to draw pictures—if you are like me, some of those will be your wonderful treasures to look back on (and show to those former children when they grow up).

When you design your photo album, you can include those cards—either glued in or put in with photo corners to match or work with your photography.

What Are You Doing for Your Photography?

Are you hiring a professional photographer? You could have friends fill in. A few years ago, disposable cameras were popular, and you could even get them personalized for weddings with your name and date printed on the outside. You may be able to find some of those in 99¢ stores—and maybe there is even a place to get them developed. But camera phones and little digital cameras may be today's equivalent. There was a movie a few years ago—*28 Days Later* (2002)—where the director edited amateur video in with the professional camera work. That could be an interesting approach to your wedding photography. Or even video—though I'm not sure how that fits into *The Paper Bride*. When you think about how obsolete so many electronic formats have become (Ever even heard of Betamax? Still have a VCR? Still listening to CDs on a stereo?)—paper may be your best choice for longevity.

If you plan to have guests take pictures, organize ahead—make sure that pictures are saved at a high enough resolution—possibly on a group website like Flickr—so that you can print the ones you like best for your album. You may at least want to go to a photographer's studio for a few formal portraits. We winged the photography for our wedding, and I looked pretty bad in the first prints I saw—always eating or looking distracted. Luckily, Richard Minsky (who founded Center for Book Arts in New York City, where we had our studio back then) came through. He'd dyed his hair magenta in a bout of punk nostalgia—and we never saw any pictures of HIM—and strangely—knowing so many bookbinders, we never had a real album (in the tradition of shoemakers' wives going barefoot, our photos are in a really ugly commercial album)—maybe I'll make one from *The Paper Bride!* (We DID make one for this book, Bryan Baker did—but it was for Amy the photographer—still going barefoot—but as soon as this book is done, I'll have time!)

Albums

If your pictures are in a variety of formats, base the size of your album on the largest—say 8" x 10" (20 x 25.5 cm)—which could go either vertical (portrait) or horizontal (landscape). Try the picture on a few backgrounds to see how much margin you would like to leave around it.

One solution to fitting a variety of format pictures into an album is to make your album square, in a size big enough for the largest format plus, say, 4" (10 cm) (the measurement is arbitrary—whatever looks good to you)—and then place photos on the squares—for small photos, you can even put more than one on a page.

Albums, like scrapbooks, need extra spine space to make up for the amount of space the addition of pictures (or whatever) will add. Think about this in terms of loose-leaf notebooks—which I used when I was in high school—when you buy them, they are triangular—but as you fill them with paper and folders, they become flat and even overstuffed by the end of the year. You could, of course, use a loose-leaf binder for an album—but that might not be so pretty. (Though you may think of a way to make that work for you—archival plastic sheets are an excellent way to protect photos).

There are many ways to make the allowance for space at the spine. If you are stitching an album, a way to do this is to use thick linen thread. Sometimes people include spacers—little folded pieces stitched between the pages, to give more space at the spine. It makes sense to pile up your photo prints and the number of pages you want so you can see how bulky your finished book will be and allow for that.

Before you make an album, decide how you will attach your photos—you can adhere them directly to the pages or use photo corners or cut slits in the pages at the corners to insert the photos. You could also make mats—one clever way to do this is to cut an X into the album page, fold it back, place your photos in the opening, and fold the corners back around it. A more standard picture mat is another approach.

You also need to decide if you want to have pictures on facing pages or just on the right side. Juxtaposition can be interesting—but spaciousness has a nice, luxurious feel.

I recommend getting cheap prints—even black-and-white photocopies—and using those to design—and then working with your real prints based on the dummy version you've made.

{ **Photos by Richard Minsky; upper right by Dikko's dad, Paul Faust.** }

Coptic Photo Album

Bryan Baker showed me a variation of Coptic binding. He calls it Ethiopian binding—and Coptic binding did start in Ethiopia, where it was an early Christian binding. Bibles are still bound that way there. Someone showed it to Bryan when he was in school in Ohio, and he made this album for Amy's wedding photos.

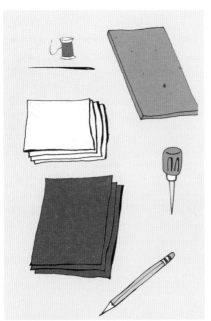

Materials

FOLDABLE, HEAVY-WEIGHT PAPER FOR INTERIOR PAGES—*at least twelve sheets (if you want to make this book as a notebook or a guest book, you may want more paper—and if you do, then you may also want to use thinner paper)*

BOARDS—*can be covered with paper or book cloth if you like (instructions on page 19) and lined with endpapers*

AWL

PENCIL

NEEDLES *(Bryan uses doll needles that he gets in craft stores—I've done other Coptic bindings with curved needles)*

LINEN THREAD *(I prefer waxed—you can wax your own with beeswax if you like—but choose a thread weight that goes with your project—if the album is small and delicate, go thinner, if it's large and chunky, go thicker. The thickness of the thread will allow more space in the spine to accommodate the bulk of the photos)*

WASTE SHEETS

1 Choose a page size that makes sense for your photos—it should be a bit larger than your photos all around. Consider using square pages so both vertical and horizontal format photos will frame well. Cut your paper and fold the signatures the same size as the covers or just a touch smaller. To fold a signature, pile up your sheets of paper, and fold in half with the grain (see page 27)—taking that path of least resistance—careful that your corners meet.

You will notice that the fore-edge (a fancy bookbinding lingo for "front edge") forms a tiny symmetrical point (if you look down on it from above)—this is because of the paper thickness. The outer sheet needs to go around the inner sheet, so the outer ends up a touch shorter.

The book you are holding has most likely been trimmed flat after it was sewn, but Knopf books have texture on the edge.

If you are using heavy paper, two sheets is enough for a signature. This book needs at least six signatures for the stitch to look interesting.

{ Bryan Baker stitched this Ethiopian Coptic album.

2 This cover stitch looks nice, but it can be tricky—so practice on a scrap a few times before you use your "good" paper. An easier way to attach your cover is to simply wrap your thread through one hole in the board two or three times (matter of personal preference—whatever looks good)—and then stitch through your wrap before going into that signature.

4 Punch holes in your cover that line up with the holes in the signatures, about 1/4" (6 mm) in from the spine's edge. Punch a second hole next to the first—another 1/4" (6 mm) in or so. These measurements are arbitrary—plan the holes for a pleasing proportional effect, as shown. Make a light pencil mark on each signature in the front lower right-hand corner to keep track of their orientation.

3 Punch holes with your awl in your signature close to the top, close to the bottom, and two toward the middle. You may like the look if they are vertically symmetrical on the spine, but it's more foolproof if they are uneven. If your holes are symmetrical, you may put in a page upside down. Bryan did this when he was demonstrating the stitch for the illustrator—and he's made hundreds of these books.

5 Cut two lengths of thread that extend from one shoulder to the opposite extended hand—or whatever length you are comfortable sewing, not too long or it will tangle. You can, alternatively, measure your signature and try to figure out your thread length by how much you'll use, but with all the stitching, be sure to allow extra.

split the thread

6 Thread each length of thread onto two needles, one on each end—and lock onto the needle, backstitching through the tail of your thread, splitting the thread, and then pushing down and pulling taut as shown.

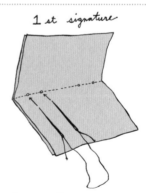

1st signature

7 Start inside your first signature and push the needles out, one length of thread centered on the two bottom holes, the other centered on the two top holes. Even out your needles—this stitch is something like lacing shoes—so keep it even, like shoelaces.

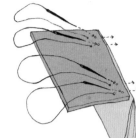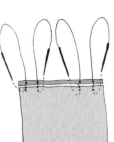

8 Now here is the interesting part: Gently push in through the edge, penetrating the side of the board, to the first hole (closest to the spine). Pivot your needle so that it tilts out of the first hole. Drop down through the second hole. Exit back out the first hole gently through the edge of your board again—veering to the side of your original stitch. Be careful not to pierce/split your thread.

9 Repeat with the other three needles, sewing into the appropriate holes.

10 Close the cover, being careful of orientation—make sure that your light pencil mark is on the bottom right, next to the cover.

11 Put your needles back into your first signature as shown. Cross them and go out again. Bryan has a cool trick to keep from piercing his thread—he uses his pinky finger to pull the one thread to the side, keeping it taut, while the other thread passes through the hole.

12 Stitch back into your board, repeating the board attachment process (steps 8–10) very carefully, laying your thread next to the thread before, so that you don't split through the board (as I did the first time I tried it—really, practice this!).

13 When you go out, add your second signature, going in, crossing through, and going out the holes. Note: This signature will have two threads crossing—the first where you started has three—the final signature will also have three, but all the inner signatures have two.

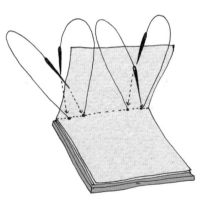

14 Now start your Coptic stitch, which reminds some people of knitting. Take your needle between your first signature and board, wrap around that stitch, and come back out. Choose which direction you want to wrap and keep that consistent. You may want to wrap from the center toward the top and bottom edge—that's what I usually do.

With his long straight doll needles, Bryan pushes in and then backs his needles out around the stitch—this way he doesn't need a curved needle, but you could use either.

Then go into your third signature. Cross threads, come out of the signature, and wrap around the stitch between the first and second signature. Always Coptic-stitch back one.

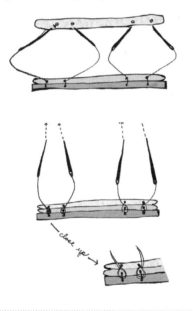

15 Add your fourth signature and repeat that process (steps 13 through 14)—this part is fun.

Keep going, adding signatures, crossing threads, Coptic-stitching around the stitch one signature back, and adding the new signature until you add your last signature. Coptic-stitch back one signature, as you have been doing.

17 When you come out through the edge of the board, Coptic-stitch back around the stitch between your last and penultimate (a fancy word for next-to-last) signatures. Then stitch back into your board, repeating that board attachment (steps 8–10)—by now you're good at it! Be careful to direct your needle to the side of your previous stitch, so that you don't split your thread or your board.

Close your book and check your tension—does the back cover close? If not, now is your chance to loosen things a little.

16 Then attach the back board, repeating the steps you used for the front board (steps 8–10), drilling your needle through the edge of the board and going in and out of the holes as before.

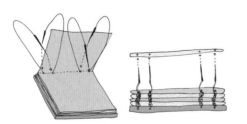

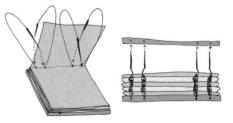

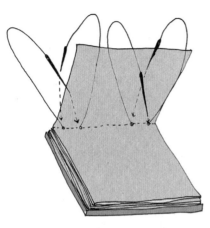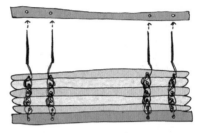

18 Stitch into your last signature and tie off your threads. Either square-knot (left over right/right over left) them together, one knot for the top threads and another for the bottom threads. OR tie off with four separate kettle stitches—loop around the thread and pull your thread through your loop, like tying off a thread when you hem a skirt, as shown.

Your first try will not be perfect (it's like a first scarf, if you are learning to knit)—if it is perfect, there is something wrong with you—you are too good. For MOST of us, it takes a few tries before it's good enough to use with fancy, expensive paper. Make a few of these with nice cheap paper to use as notebooks, and when you are happy with your tension and feel you understand it, use the good stuff to make your photo album.

19 Arrange your photos and adhere them to the book with photo corners, or use photo-safe glue sticks or float them with archival double-stick tape. And (as always) burnish well, protecting photos with clean waste sheets.

NOTE: This binding also works for guest books, favors, honeymoon journals, and gifts for your attendants. You could even make the covers from postcards of your honeymoon location (How to Make Books, my first how-to book, includes a one-needle Coptic binding with postcard covers).

Flag book Photo Album

Alternatively you can make a great photo album from Hedi Kyle's Flag Book which I showed you for the Flag Book Cookbook (page 70). Just mount your photos onto the pages and attach the pages to the concertina spine as you did for the recipe cards.

Afterword
Paper
Anniversary

*P*aper anniversaries didn't sound like much fun when I first heard about them. It seemed like you'd have to be married forever before you got anything good.

But really by the time you've reached gold, well, that's a long time away—will you be able to enjoy the gold? As long as you've got your health!

But now I have spent half my life working with paper—it is what I love—so I have greater appreciation for the paper anniversary. Plus I know of some $50/sheet handmade papers—though I seldom get to buy them.

I also think that the first year of marriage is a serious accomplishment and deserves real celebration. After the intensity and pressure of making a wedding, the first year is a relief. Time flies when you're having fun, and suddenly you've been married for a whole year.

Save the ephemera from your first year together—the concert tickets, the foreign money—those great little printed French pastry bags, the diner place mats—and do something nice with them.

{ Susan Happersett collaged the cover of an old book that she filled with a pocket accordion (page 122) for her paper anniversary memento.

Memento Accordion

This pocket accordion book re-uses the cover of an existing book. Or cover boards (page 19)—or use raw board for the covers.

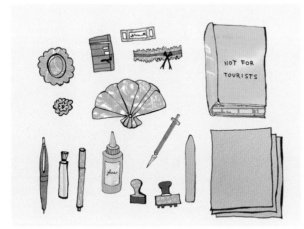

Materials

EPHEMERA *from your first year of marriage*

SMALL HARDCOVER BOOK TO REUSE

FOLDABLE, HEAVY-WEIGHT PAPER

BONE FOLDER

X-ACTO KNIFE

GLUE

COLLAGE MATERIAL

MARKERS, RUBBER STAMPS, ETC., *for embellishment*

1 Save all the ticket stubs, coasters, and other bits of interesting ephemera from your first-year travels and adventures—even ordinary computer-printed movie stubs may have some nostalgic charm when you look back at them in a few years—but if you travel, the most ordinary bits of paper are exotic.

2 Find a hardback book that you'd like to reuse—with a good sturdy cover. You can leave the cover as is, or collage the cover, as Susan Happersett did for the one in the picture on page 120. Gently remove the inside of the book, cutting out the pages and slicing through the threads with an X-Acto knife.

3 Measure the cover. That plus a bit more for your pocket—a few inches (a few centimeters)—will be the height of your accordion. The cover's width should a little bigger than your page width. This book works best with an even number of pages.

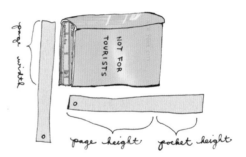

4 If you can't buy long enough paper, you can add another piece with a paper hinge—which is how we always make our accordions. This can be very subtle or as interesting or as decorative as you like.

First fold both pieces into the accordion size you need.

For a self-hinge, plan for an extra 1/2" (13 mm) or so on one piece and use that extra to attach to the other piece with glue or double-stick tape.

Or use another paper—possibly something collage-like—it does not need to be as tall as the page (think about door hinges)—just enough for strength and structure. Try out some hinge ideas on scraps to see what works with your design.

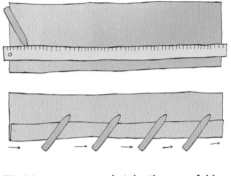

5 Measure your pocket depth, score, fold up, and burnish. Then unfold while you fold the accordion.

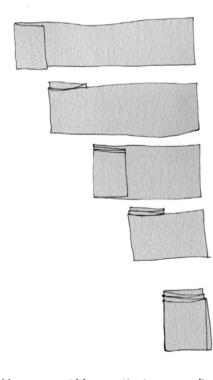

6 Fold your page width, repeating in an accordion, folding only one paper thickness at a time.

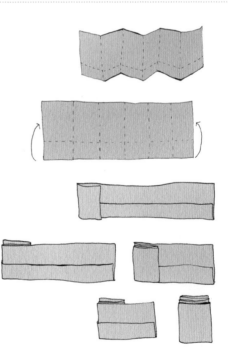

7 Once you have folded the accordion, burnish well, unfold, fold up the pocket, and carefully refold the accordion.

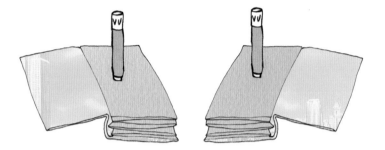

8 Glue both accordion ends to the covers of your book—this accordion should not be as thick as your spine—to allow space for putting things in the pockets.

Collage with ephemera and embellish the pockets and pages—if you use acrylic paint, the pages will stick together, since acrylic adheres with a weird chemical bond—so you'll need to rub the painted pages with wax. Dorland's Wax is popular for this purpose—you could try beeswax for a different-looking, nice-smelling alternative. Or use watercolor or gouache to paint your pages—they won't stick. Susan sealed the outer sides of the pockets so nothing would fall out. A thin strip of double-stick tape or a glue stick would do the trick.

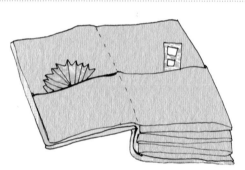

9 Put an item or two into each pocket—and, if you like, in the last pocket put another paper gift—like tickets to something special or a gift certificate to come to Purgatory Pie Press for a paper present (Jessica who works at McNally Jackson, my favorite NYC bookstore, gave that to her husband for their first anniversary).

Appendix

Paste + Paste Paper

Homemade wheat paste??! Why would anyone want to make paste? Because it's easy, cheap, archival, and it disappears when it dries (IF you use THIN coats). Dikko and I have been guest artists in towns where there isn't an art store or even a Staples—but unbleached flour is easy to find in the grocery store. (In Los Cruces, New Mexico, we also found the most delicious peanuts—grocery stores can be some of the best tourist experiences.)

You can color paste to use for your own decorative paste paper.

To make your own paste:

1 **Combine 1 part unbleached flour and 6 parts water. For example, use 2 teaspoons (4g/10ml) of unbleached flour to 4 tablespoons or 1/4 cup (60ml) water.**

2 **Stir until milky. Cook and stir until the mixture thickens and turns translucent.**

3 **I make small quantities in plastic take-out containers in the microwave. The microwave is slow for large amounts. You can cook and stir in a pot—but seriously this stuff scorches—so use a wooden spoon, stir constantly, and don't look away or wander off. I met someone once who used a double boiler (do you have one of those?). You might be able to use a slow-cooker or a Rice-O-Matic to cook paste.**

4 **Wheat paste lasts for a couple days in the refrigerator. But, since it takes about a minute to make about 1/4 cup (60 ml) (enough to line many envelopes), I suggest that you make tiny batches. Just make more if you run out. Wheat paste isn't sticky, but it works well to adhere paper to paper.**

5 **Always use this paste very sparingly. It won't be sticky at first, so you can reposition what you are pasting. It adhere as it dries. If you are pasting a large area, you'll need to cover it with a layer of clean waste sheets and dry the piece under weight so that the moisture does not wrinkle your paper. Keep changing waste sheets as it dries. That's not much fun. I use wheat paste for small areas: for collage, labels, or tipping (pasting the edges of) bookplates.**

> ### ✦ A QUICK AMERICAN HOME EC LESSON ✦
>
> 3 teaspoons = 1 tablespoon,   And metric!
> so 2 teaspoons to 4 tablespoons   1 teaspoon = 5ml
> = 1:6 ratio   1 tablespoon = 15 ml
> (AND 4 tablespoons = 1/4 cup,   1 cup = 250 ml
> 8 tablespoons = 1/2 cup,
> 16 tablespoons = 1 cup)
>
> *Remember this for the quiz!!*

To make your own paste paper:

1 Make a large quantity of paste. Separate your paste into several containers, the way you'd separate icing to decorate cupcakes or cookies or cakes. Add color to each one—you can use powdered pigment or a squirt of acrylic or liquid watercolor—or even metallic powders—or fine glitter.

2 Prepare you paper by lightly brushing with water—or misting with a spray bottle. Brush the colored paste onto the paper. Using forks or combs or pieces of wood type or brushes, try some patterns. Experiment—it's a lot like finger paint—just keep your layers very thin. When you like the effect, repeat that to make enough paper for your project.

3 If you are using this paper for an envelope lining, make it in large sheets and then cut your shapes out of it instead of trying to paint the smaller liner-size papers. Some paper curls when wet—you can tape it to a board before you start. When it's dry, you can put it between clean waste sheets and weight it down. Weighting under a rug for a few days works well—but don't trip on the uneven surface.

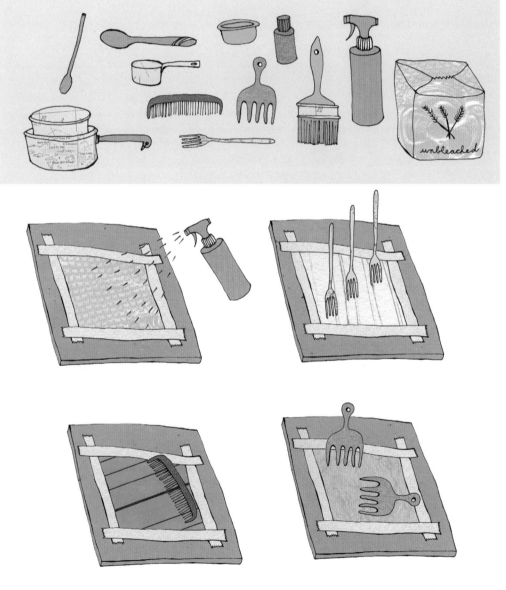

THE PAPER BRIDE
HANDWRITING GUIDE

Of course a dip pen and a bottle of ink can be nice to work with—but even Jennifer King, who does our calligraphy (and lettered this page) uses markers for her informal style. Start out at your favorite art store or stationer and try out some pens. When you find the one you like, buy several, so you aren't stuck with a dried out pen in the middle of the night addressing envelopes.

Feel free to try other writing styles—or make up your own. Georgia Luna loves typography and lettering and had a great time making the place cards (page 98) and map (page 60). Architects also learn a great style of drafting lettering—maybe you can find a student architect to address envelopes for you.

Practice makes perfect! 1 2 3 4 5 6 7 8 9 0

a b c d e f g h i j k l m

a b c d e f g h i j k l m

n o p q r s t u v w x y z

n o p q r s t u v w x y z

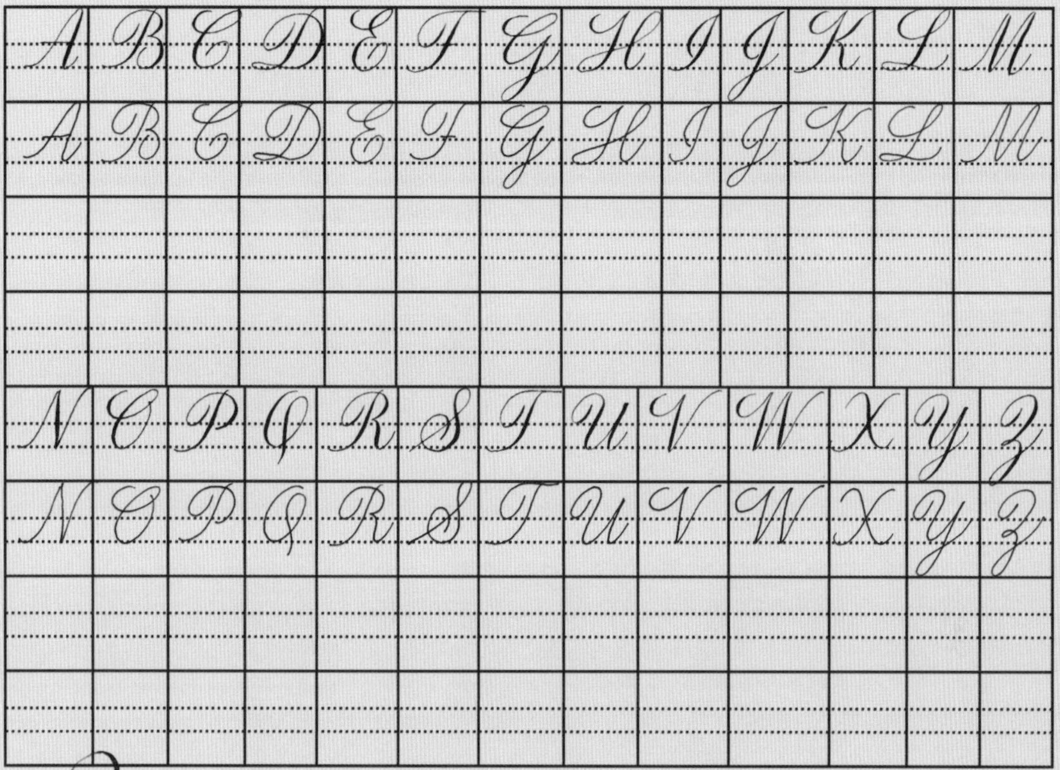

A B C D E F G H I J K L M

A B C D E F G H I J K L M

N O P Q R S T U V W X Y Z

N O P Q R S T U V W X Y Z

HOW TO ADDRESS AN ENVELOPE

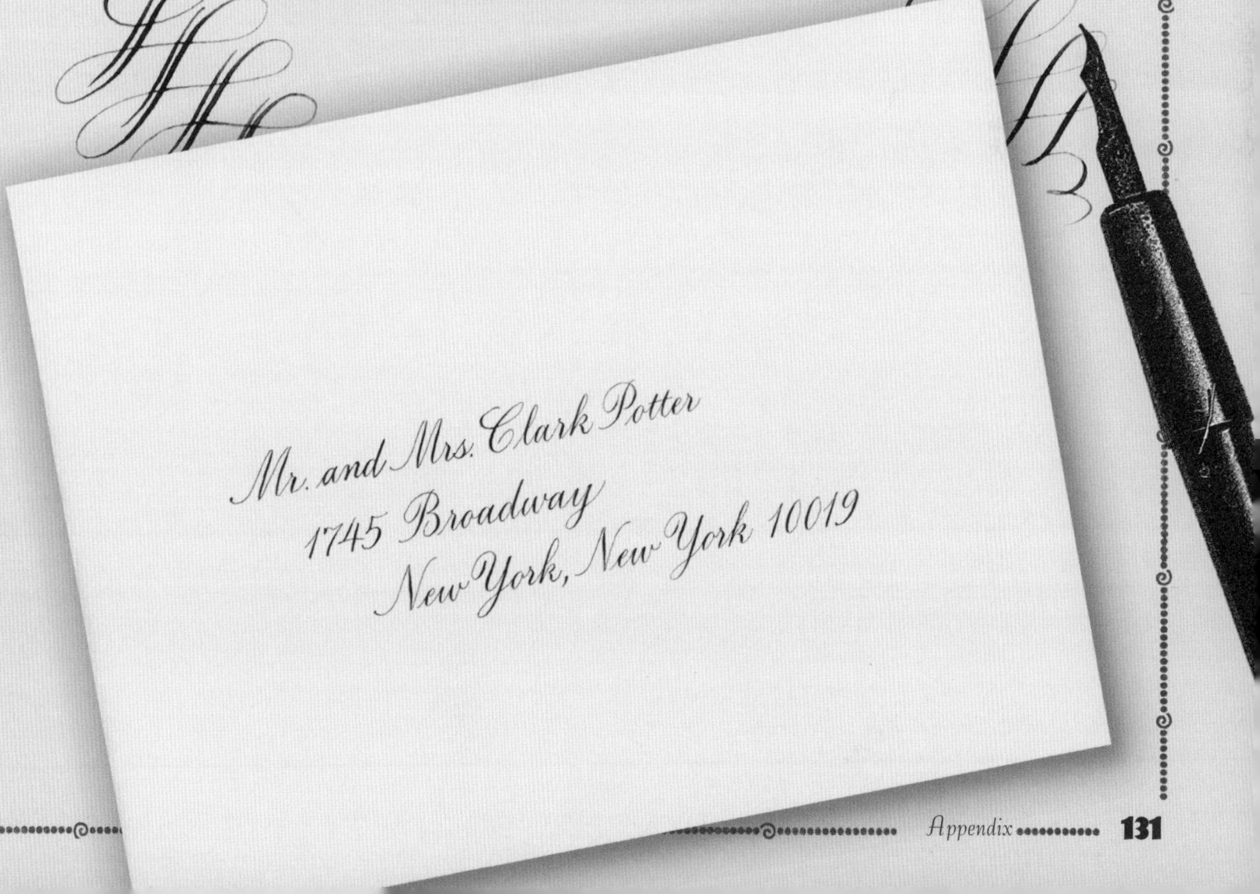

Mr. and Mrs. Clark Potter
1745 Broadway
New York, New York 10019

Templates

* Via photocopier, enlarge these to the size of your choice. Try them on scrap paper first and alter the shapes to make your own designs.

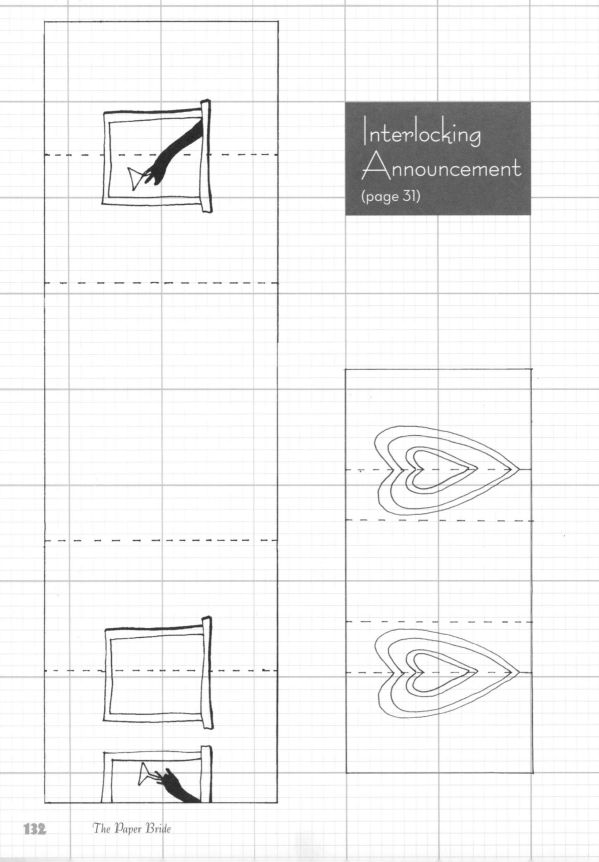

Interlocking
Announcement
(page 31)

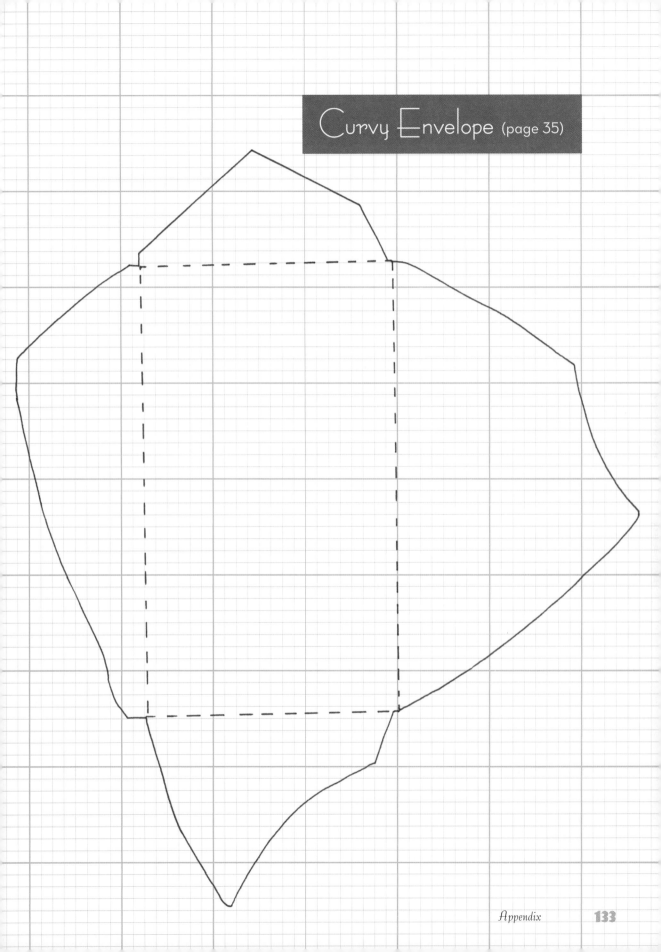

Curvy Envelope (page 35)

Templates

Cake Box (page 103)

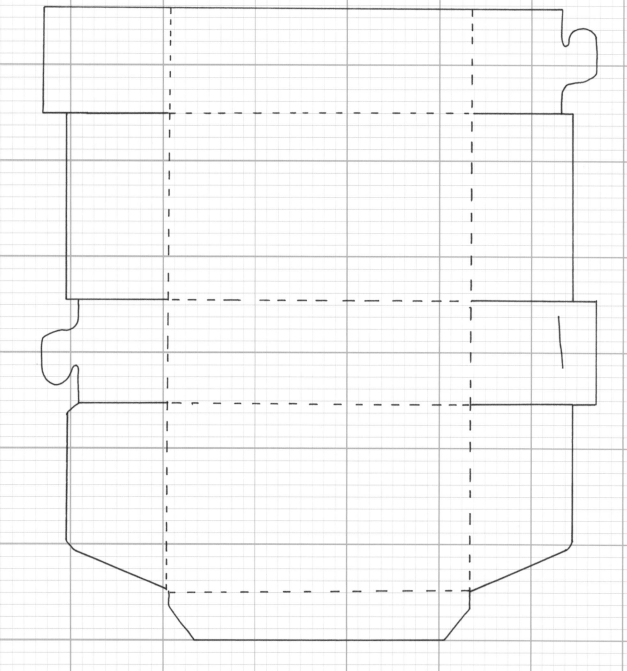

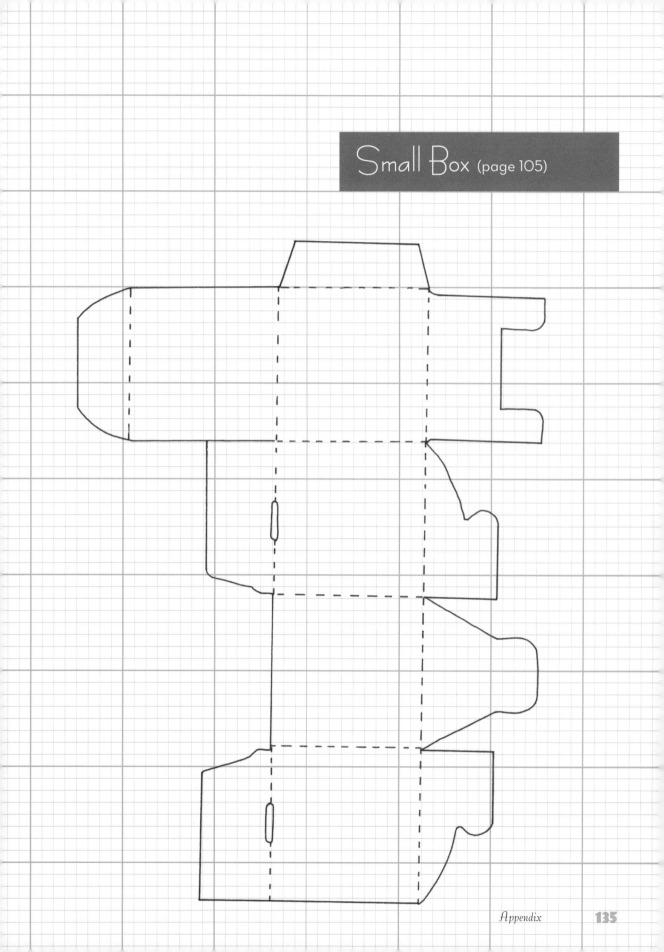

Small Box (page 105)

Templates

Napkin Ring (page 99)

Coaster (page 104)

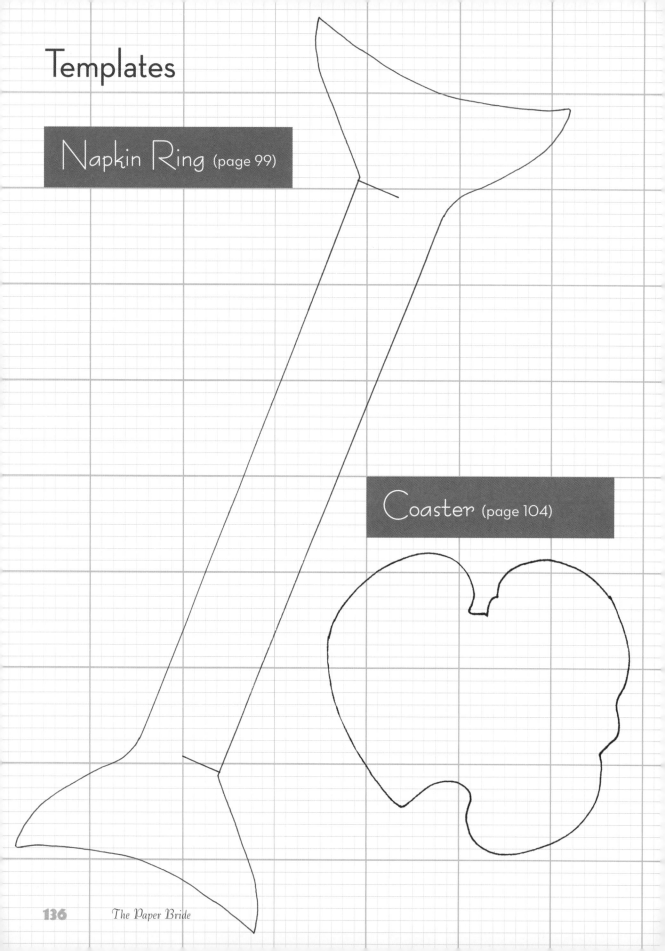

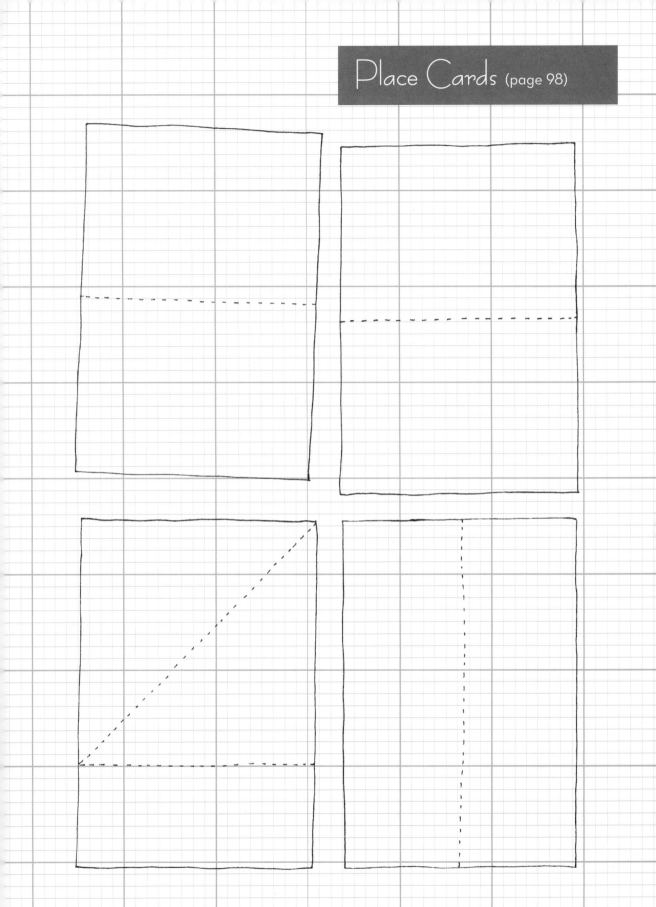

Templates

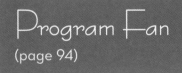

Program Fan
(page 94)

Cake Topper (page 102)

Resources

Letterpress

Purgatory Pie Press
purgatorypiepress.com

Bremelo Press
*Lynda Sherman, our former helper,
has a letterpress studio in Seattle.*
1426 South Jackson Street, Seattle WA 98144
bremelopress.com : 206-713-4080

Paper makers

Carriage House Paper
245 Kent Ave, Brooklyn NY 11211
carriagehousepaper.com
800-669-8781 : 718-559-7857

**Katie Macgregor
Macgregor Handmade Paper**
P.O. Box 70, Whiting ME 04691
207-733-0991

Women's Studio Workshop
PO Box 489, Rosendale NY 12472
wsworkshop.org

Engraving

Nancy Sharon Collins
nancysharoncollinsstationer.com

Rubber Stamps

Hero Rubber Stamps
HeroArts.com

Supplies

Talas
talasonline.com : 212-219-0770

Royalwood
royalwoodltd.com : 800-526-1630

Kate's Paperie
katespaperie.com : 800-809-9880

NY Central Art Supply
62 Third Ave, NYC 10003
nycentralart.com : 800-950-61111

Paper Source
PaperSource.com

My students recommend:

Ben Franklin Crafts
benfranklinstores.com : 800-992-9307

Beverly's
beverlys.com : 800-449-2148 : *info@beverlys.com*

Blick
dickblick.com/categories/bookmaking : 800-828-4548

Flax
FlaxArt.com

Daniel Smith
danielsmith.com : 800-426-6740

De Medici Ming Fine Paper •
1222 1st Ave Ste A, Seattle, WA 98101 : 206-624-1983

Jo-Ann Fabric and Craft Stores
joann.com : 888-739-4120

Michaels
michaels.com/paper-crafts : 800-642-4235
Martha Stewart's bookarts supplies are a high point.

Pearl Paint
pearlpaint.com : 800-451-7327

Utrecht
utrechtart.com/Paper-Boards/Printmaking-Paper/
800-223-9132

Books

The DIY Wedding: Celebrate Your Day Your Way
by Kelly Bare and Natalie Zee Drieu
(San Francisco: Chronicle Books, 2007)
I found this when I was looking at books for interesting approaches to paperback covers—and so wish I'd had it when I was doing my own wedding!

Miss Manners on Painfully Proper Weddings
by Judith Martin
(New York: Crown Publishing, 1995)
Miss Manners is worth reading for the laughs alone. She deals with wedding-related information in most of her books and many of her columns—this book is specific to the topic!

Maria McBride has done wedding books and has a lovely website: **MariaMcBride.com**

The Perfect Wedding
by Maria McBride
(Harper Collins, 1996)

The Perfect Wedding Reception
by Maria McBride
(Collins Living, 2000)

If you love making the things in this book, you'll need my other two books—many of their projects could work for your wedding (with a bit of your own imagination and creativity).

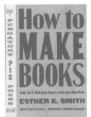

How to Make Books
Fold, Cut, & Stitch Your Way to a One-of-a-Kind Book
(New York: Potter Craft, 2007)

Magic Books & Paper Toys
Flip Books, E-Z Pop-Ups and Other Paper Playthings to Amaze & Delight
(New York: Potter Craft, 2008)

Design

STEVEN HELLER
has written bookshelves full of design books. His **Print Magazine** *blog is a great place to start:*
The Daily Heller
hellerbooks.com

ELLEN LUPTON's
design books are also excellent resources.
EllenLupton.com

Classes

You can study with me at **Cooper Union** *or take calligraphy there.*
Cooper.edu

Saturday the 6th of September, when I was in the midst of writing this book, we were awakened by a loud roaring crashing noise that kept going and going. Dikko ran into the living room and found a pile of pale grey, band-aid pink, chartreuse, and dark turquoise broken dishes, Russell Wright Steubenville. Our glass front Ikea dish cabinet had broken off the wall, hit a cluttered counter, then a sideboard, crushing what it hit. At first I had a feeling of shocked relief. It wasn't the girls' room. We weren't hurt. Our computers weren't damaged. It wasn't national news.

That Russell Wright pottery was our wedding china. We bought a whole set of it combining a bunch of $10 and $20 checks we got as wedding presents in 1980. The store where we bought it had a deal that you could replace broken pieces at a low price. They'd been out of business for decades.

It was too good for everyday, we always saved it—low fire pottery chips. We used it on holidays, when we were entertaining. The day after this small disaster, I poured Dikko's coffee into one of the dark turquoise cups that survived. I drank my coffee from a pink one. All the chartreuse and grey cups had broken.

I want to dedicate this book in part to the memory of Russell Wright (and his wife and collaborator Mary). Dikko, Lissi, and I designed this book around the colors of those dishes.

And I want to encourage you, in your marriage, to not save things for good, but to enjoy them in the daily life that will be your real happily ever after . . .

Thanks to all the brides (& grooms and mothers-of-the-brides) who took the plunge and came to Purgatory Pie Press for your wedding stationery. I hope that no matter what you are living happily ever after, richer rather than poorer—and in health!

And thanks to Richard Minsky for our wedding pix, and to Nancy Picchi, Stan Pinkwas and Miriam Schaer, Susan Cohen, Ezra and Louise Smith, Paula Michaels and Clyde Smith, Gloria and John Happersett, Paul and Patty and Betty and Sherry Faust, Felicity and Murphy, Alice Austin, Amy and Josh, Kyle Forester, Alex Campos, Phil Zimmerman, Joshua Schrier and Eve Eisenstadt, Deb Wood and Dave Konopka, Laura Reddick and Daniel Roode, Laura Carmelita Bellmont, Linda Montano, Harvey Spiller, Martha Wilson, Jane Penner and Diana Slotznick.

Thanks to Lissi Erwin, Liz Zanis, and Amy Kalyn Sims, and Dikko Faust for making this book with me.

Thanks

And to Susan Springer Anderson for the paper dress, Bryan Baker for the Ethiopian album, Ashley Soliman SmashleySoliman.com for the paper flowers and headdresses, Jennifer King for the fan, programs & handwriting, Susan Happersett LazySusanCollages.com for the accordion memento and collages, Georgia Luna for the ringbox book and coasters, and Polly Faust for the papercaketoppers.

Thanks to Kim Muench for lending her car and to Matt Danzico for chauffering The Paper Bride's Dress.

And at Random House, thanks again to the excellent sales team and thanks to Lauren & Shawna & Christina & Melissa & Rosy & Erin & Erica & Betty & Victoria & Amy & Isa & Thom & Chi Ling & La Tricia & Alice & Katherine & Donna & Alison & Kim & Alexis & Marysarah.

Esther K Smith

is the author of *How to Make Books* and *Magic Books & Paper Toys*. She collaborates with hand-typographer *Dikko Faust* and other artists and writers to make limited editions and artistbooks at Purgatory Pie Press in New York City. Solo exhibits include the Metropolitan Museum of Art and London's Victoria & Albert Museum. Their wedding stationery with their limited editons is in rare books/ephemera collections at the New York Public Library and Stanford University. Their token themed wedding stationery was featured at the Museum of the City of New York's NEW YORK GETS MARRIED exhibition.

PurgatoryPiePress.com ❦ ThePaperBride@gmail.com

Photo: Karen Detrick

Amy Kalyn Sims

majored in Photography and Graphic Design at the Savannah College of Art and Design. She first studied photography with renowned Florida photographer David Woods. Known for her fine art photography as well as her still-life, food, and portrait work, she had her first solo show at Bok Tower Gardens (Lake Wales, Florida) in 1997. *Clients include:* Clarkson Potter, Country Home, Fitness, Good Housekeeping, Mud Puddle Books, Crafts, Walk Up Records, and Wine Spectator.

Amy would like to thank her husband, Joshua Levy, and her ever supportive family, Anna and Donald Lewis and Evelyn Fields.

❦ AmyKalynSims.com

Lissi Erwin

is the Art Director/Proprietor of Splendid Corp., a small design studio in Brooklyn, NY. Splendid Corp. brings together the old and the new for a crafty vernacular design aesthetic. Lissi has designed books such as *The Best of LCD: The Art and Writing of WFMU*, *Pure Country*, and *Cassette From My Ex*.

Lissi would like to thank Esther and Dikko for bringing letterpress and the joys of ink, paper, and eclectic typefaces back into her life. An immense hug and kiss to fiancé Ryan Murphy for bearing with her through the many late nights married to her computer. Ship's Ahoy!

❦ SplendidCorp.com

Liz Zanis

graduated from the Rhode Island School of Design with her Bachelor's Degree of Fine Art in Illustration. She traffics in eavesdroppings and family histories, often appropriating them for small object-based autobiographical work. Her nights and weekends are spent wrestling screens, plates, and type while printing tiny prints which may or may not become limited edition artist's books. Her work has been exhibited at two libraries, one print studio, one workshop, one Flux Factory, one print center, two museums, and one center for book arts. ❦ LizzZanis.com

Index

Copyright © 2009 by Esther K. Smith
Typographic illustrations copyright © 2009 by Dikko Faust/Purgatory Pie Press
Photographs copyright © 2009 by Amy Kalyn Sims
Illustrations copyright © 2009 by Liz Zanis

All rights reserved.

Published in the United States by Potter Craft, an imprint of the
Crown Publishing Group, a division of Random House, Inc., New York.
www.clarksonpotter.com
www.pottercraft.com

POTTER CRAFT and colophon is a registered trademark of Random House, Inc.

Library of Congress Cataloging-in-Publication Data

Smith, Esther K.
  The paper bride / Esther K. Smith. — 1st ed.
    p. cm.
  ISBN 978-0-307-40710-8
  1. Paper work. 2. Wedding decorations. 3. Wedding stationery.
  4. Weddings—Equipment and supplies. I. Title.
  TT870.S57154 2009
  745.92'6—dc22

                                    2009016019

Printed in China

Design by Esther K. Smith/Purgatory Pie Press
& Lissi Erwin/Splendid Corp.

Collages on p.2, p.142, + p.144 by Susan Happersett / LazySusanCollages.com

10 9 8 7 6 5 4 3 2 1

First Edition

our picture here

BOWL

This was taken at Proposal Rock so called because your father proposed to your mother here

NAME AND ADDRESS HERE
•olio
PLACE
•01
STAMP
•1
HERE
•0
•olio
CARD